SUCCESS WORKS
20 Stories of a Journey to the Top

SUCCESS WORKS - 20 Stories of a Journey to the Top

GMCP Edition

Copyright © 2018 by Global Mentoring Center Publishing. All rights reserved.

Published by The Global Mentoring Center

Editor in Chief: Elie Saba

All Rights Reserved. No part of this publication may be produced in any form or by any means, mechanical or electronic, including photocopy and recording, or by any information storage and retrieval system, without the permission in writing from the author or publisher; exceptions are made for brief excerpts used in published reviews.

This publication is designed to provide accurate and authoritative information in regard to the subject matter covered. It is sold with the understanding that the publisher is not engaged in rendering legal, accounting, or other professional services. If legal advice or other expert assistance is required, the services of a competent professional should be sought.

Ordering Information

To order additional copies, contact your local bookstore or visit www. globalmentoringcenter.com

Library of Congress Cataloging in Publication Data

Multiple Authors

Success Works – 20 Stories of a Journey to the Top

ISBN 978-0-9996791-7-3

1. Success 2. Motivational 3. Self-Help 4. Self-Esteem

Global Mentoring Center Publishing
9322, 3rd Avenue #460, Brooklyn NY 11209 * 917-515-6803
Printed in the United States of America
First Printing: December 2018

DEDICATION

This book has been lovingly prepared to best serve men and women worldwide who have been through life-altering experiences and reminding them that they are not alone. There is always a light at the end of the tunnel.

FOREWORD BY BERT OLIVA

In today's world where we are bombarded with sound bites and take social media posts as fact, it's hard to find truly worthwhile information sources that actually help you to become more successful. This book is one of those few meaningful works. It is an amazing collection of stories that inspire the soul and feed the mind with strategies to help in everyday living.

Many people have become successful but do not know exactly how they did it. In this collection, Orly Amor has used her unique talent to bring together thought leaders and business experts to share their wealth of knowledge and pass their strategies on to those of us who are willing to take the information in and use it.

This book provides a valuable window to the journey that all entrepreneurs take to success. It outlines the challenges, the lessons, and insights each person faced and what inspired them to keep going.

This book is meant for those people who are ready to take action and make significant leaps forward. I have had the opportunity to help, coach, and transform top leaders into using their potential and becoming the best leaders they can be. And this book is a tool that I can implement into my programs and growth strategies for my students.

Orly has been a special person in my life and the lives of many across the world. I know she has put her heart into this book for you to enjoy and advance in your life. Read it with an open heart and a desire for growth and let your transformation begin.

Bert Oliva

Leadership & Human Behavior Expert

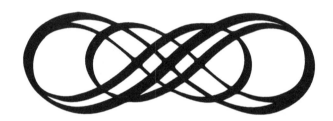

CONTENTS

DEDICATION III

FOREWORD BY BERT OLIVA...........................IV

HOW TO HEAL YOURSELF
- NOTES OF A HEALER BIKER 1

SEARCHING FOR SUCCESS...............................9

SHIFTING SANDS IN THE STORM OF SUCCESS....17

FINDING MY SPATULA 23

LAVUE BOUTIQUE 31

FROM DEVASTATION TO RECOUPMENT AND BEYOND
....37

AWAKEN - MY JOURNEY TO SELF-LOVE AND
SELF-ACCEPTANCE 45

I AWAKEN AS I SLEEP 51

THE SPOON 57

HOW I LEARNED TO SERVE NOT SELL 63

THE LIFE-CHANGING POWER OF WRITING A BOOK
....69

vii

GETTING TO THE BOTTOM 77

LEADER OF THE PACK: 83

HOW A SINGLE DAD OF FIVE LED HIS KIDS, HIS BUSINESS AND HIMSELF FROM DISASTER TO SUCCESS. 83

LOOK UP, GROW UP, SHOW UP 91

WHAT IS YOUR THOUGHT PATTERN? 97

WHEN LOVE IS NOT ENOUGH 101

A LAWYER… JUST LIKE YOU - 107

A GIRL'S JOURNEY IN THE FOOTSTEPS OF HER MENTOR 107

THE RIPPLE EFFECT 113

FAT GIRL CHRONICLES 121

WHEN OPPORTUNITY KNOCKS 129

1
HOW TO HEAL YOURSELF
- NOTES OF A HEALER BIKER

CSONGOR DANIEL

About the Author:

Csongor Daniel is an internationally recognized Bioenergy Healer, one the leading teachers of this method, with more than 25 years of experience and 3 published books behind him. His latest title is *Bioenergy Healing: Simple Techniques for Reducing Pain and Restoring Health through Energetic Healing* (Skyhorse Publishing, 2016). The method is a part of integrative healing and depends upon the energy of the body to heal itself and does not require surgery or pain-killing drugs. It is open to anyone to learn.

Csongor always welcomes new healing challenges and invitations to teach anywhere in the world.

You may join his free Long-Distance Group Healing here:
https://www.facebook.com/longdistancebioenergyhealing/
Website: www.csongordaniel.com

How to Heal Yourself - Notes of a Healer Biker

"How can you keep partying every damn night?" asked my dad. "All you do is pursue pleasure! Don't you ever get tired of it?"

"When am I going to do it if not now?!" was my smartass answer, which pissed my dad off even more. Of course, I was only 20 and that was my main existence in our small town in Yugoslavia. My life was about to end as it was. I wanted to put in as much partying, riding motorcycles, and chasing girls, as I could handle before leaving for the mandatory military service. I had no other plans, directions or aspirations whatsoever.

Military was like prison for the free spirit I had become. By then I had traversed half of Europe on my souped up moped. All of a sudden, I lost my home, my girlfriend, and my freedom. A grueling 13 months later I was back home eager to continue where I left off.

In that short amount of time, everything had changed: my buddies had gone to work or college, the town was transformed, and I had responsibilities. "College or work – that is your choice!" said my dad. None appealed to me, but I ended up studying engineering, which fulfilled my logical/ technical nature, yet still left a gap in my direction-seeking mind.

Half way through my studies, my dad's friend visited and

3

introduced us to bioenergy healing. It was mind-boggling to learn to feel the energy that surrounds our bodies and pervades the universe. My dad, with his chemist mind thought it was funny. To me it was serious - a sensation I felt my entire life, now explained.

All of a sudden, everything changed. I started playing with this energy, feeling it, seeing it. I didn't know what to do with it yet, but it was still amazing!

When my marathon runner friend complained about his ankle pain, I gave it a try to stop it with my newfound skill. It worked! The pain vanished. By the time my mom complained about her back a few weeks later, I had enough confidence to attempt to fix it. I will never forget what happened next. To our astonishment, as I was pulling the "bad energy" out of her back, she started leaning back. As I moved my hand forward, she moved forward. After a few more back and forth moves, I asked my mom what the hell she was doing. "Nothing. What are you doing???" she asked. "I don't know! What are you doing?" I replied. We were freaking out and laughing at the same time. We realized that I could move her without touching her - an ability called psychokinesis.

The same night I went out with my friends and told them what happened. Naturally, they were all laughing – until I showed them. They were moving like palm trees in a hurricane! By the end of the night we were betting in beer on who would move and who wouldn't. The entire pub was into it. Now I really had to take this seriously! I had to learn to use these powers properly, but I knew of no other person doing or teaching this.

What followed was a chain of events that seemed like a coincidence. First, I saw on the news an aerial photo of hundreds of people waiting in line to see Zdenko Domancic, a Croatian healer on a small Adriatic island. The footage showed him working on them and manipulating their energy in such fashion that they were moving back and forth and even bending! My attempts to find him were futile. But I knew there was hope to understand what I was doing.

A week later my marathoner friend brought me an article about a professor in Belgrade measuring the energy fields of the body. I was able to join him and after testing me, he pulled me aside, looked me in the eyes and told me to change my profession – I was born to be a healer.

Then he grabbed me by my hand and an hour later introduced me to the creator of one of the most powerful healing methods on the planet: Mr. Domancic!

Naturally, I studied the Bioenergy Healing method with him. A year later I was holding both my engineering diploma and my Bioenergy Healer certificate in my hands. In a short time, I had more than thirty patients a day and was successfully healing anything from simple headaches to the most complicated medical conditions. I was making more than both my parents together! I was only 25. I was still riding motorcycles, having fun and working a fulfilling job. Life was peachy.

The first days of the Yugoslav war caught me as I was visiting my aunt in America. Suddenly I was thrown back in time feeling like my army days. This time not only had I lost my home, but I lost my country!

Realizing that none of my diplomas were accepted in the U. S., I had to start from scratch. With borrowed money I bought a motorcycle to deliver pizza on it. For my next job I was a Japanese Teppan chef. Later a massage therapist, massage instructor, T'ai Chi instructor, personal trainer…

While in Yugoslavia it took stopping one headache for the entire street to know about it the next day, the U.S. wasn't so open to this type of treatment. Starting from scratch meant literally that. I decided to learn better English, learn to use a computer, learn to type, and write a book on Biotherapy – all at once. Four years later my first book was published– just a month before my first daughter was born and just a week after I broke my femur in a wakeboarding accident. There I was again – starting anew. My first book was heavy on science, the physics underlying the method and other complementary energy treatments. Despite the doctors' prediction, not only did I walk before the 6-month forecast, but I was teaching T'ai Chi a mere month and a half later – just by working on my own energy.

When my dad visited a few months later he put his hand on my shoulder and said "You were right. That was the time to party and have fun. Not anymore!" I took that as another motivation from above (he was quite tall!) and decided to dispute my own former philosophy.

Today, I still build and ride my motorcycles, still heal people, just published my third book, have two beautiful daughters, and yes, I still party! I even took it to the next level: Not too long ago, I rode my bike in the Alps with my healer daughter on the back, traveling half way through Europe on our way to the next metropolis where I would teach my seminars on Bioenergy Healing. Some would say that I am still in pursuit of pleasure! Ladies and gentlemen, dad, to me this is success!

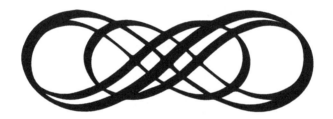

2

SEARCHING FOR SUCCESS

DR. JULEE HAFNER:

About the Author:

Julee holds a Ph.D. in Leadership from The Chicago School of Professional Psychology, a M.S. in Communication from Towson University, and a B.A. in English from the University of Pittsburgh. She is John Maxwell certified as a speaker and coach, D.I.S.C. certified, and a President's club member of Sandler Sales Training.

After spending over 20 years in the communication field, working with professionals, helping them to convey their message, build effective active listening skills, and improve constructive feedback strategies, Julee knows what truly drives professionals.

Julee understands that Human Capital is every company's most important asset. She is the Founder & CEO, (that's

Communication Effectiveness Officer), of **wehaf2talk**, a company committed to the development of professionals through workshops, seminars, and executive coaching. She uses communication strategies to build stronger personal relationships in individuals, and within teams to achieve company performance goals.

As a Communication Strategist who partners with executives and solopreneurs to grow their personal and professional brands, Julee's audiences have fun learning how to communicate with style, stay positive while confronting tough communication situations, and work more constructively together to solve problems

Website: www.DrJuleeHafner.com.

SEARCHING FOR SUCCESS

December is the time to reassess about the ending year. I was no different; I reflected every year. I asked myself several burning questions like, "How was the past year- did I have enough highlights? And, "What progress did I make toward my goals?"

At the end of that fateful year, I felt these old questions come to mind. I worried about my answers and results. I thought hard, as emotions flooded my mind. But the word success wasn't there. This past year had been really hard. My Mother had died. My business had been inconsistent. Things were in flux; I could feel that nothing was the way it should be. Maybe it was the holidays. I was unsettled, and I needed to figure this out. Was I really successful?

Sure, I could give the simple answer... But, this time that was too easy. I needed to know. *Success* was how I wanted to describe the past year, but it didn't feel right. What was *success*, really?

I thought about others' successes, but that didn't help. Maybe it was the number of cars, or houses they had. Or, it was financial worth- the money in the bank. But, for others, retiring early, and travelling... Whatever it was, I didn't have a definition that fit me. Nothing, I thought, was right.

So, what next? Success was a worthy but moving target. Would I measure up, or complete my rite of passage? I wanted to know. I looked to wiser people and did a bit of research to know how other people defined it. Guess what?

There was no clear consensus. Everywhere I looked, no one agreed. Some defined it as working toward a goal. Some about the money you had. Others suggested your job, role, or position that made you a success. It might be about your character, or your values. Well, I could accept all that. I had always been goal-oriented, tried to live a good life, and give to others. But maybe, there was a bit more to it.

The more I thought, the more I wondered. Was I really successful?

Surely, that wasn't all there was to it. It seemed to be everyone's dream, yet for me, I never thought of myself as successful. I was helping people rehabilitate from medical disabilities. Was this success, or when was I going to achieve it?

By now, I was deep in thought. I thought of examples of people I helped that year. From Richard, I saved from a kitchen fire that his wife had started by evacuating him outside, to Laura that I taught to read. She resumed reading Stephen King horror novels following her gunshot injury. Not my idea of a way to pass the time, but to each her own.

Then there was Misty, recovering from a brain aneurysm. She was worried how she would raise her children with her deficits. She worked hard to recover simple skills everyone takes for granted, like tying your shoes, or writing your name. Her biggest worry though, was that her 4-year-old would not learn to tell time "properly" because the school clocks were all digital. She did re-learn time-telling with an analog clock, so she could teach her daughter.

Then there was Max, a 91-year-old artist. When I met him,

I really thought he had some dementia. We began our work. Then he said, "Did you see that?" My back was to the door, and no, I didn't see anything. But, I played along. "What did you see, I asked?" He said, "I think saw a squirrel." I believed he might be hallucinating, but before I could respond, he said, "There it went again!" I had him stay seated while I investigated. How I get myself into these weird situations, I thought. I crept downstairs. I looked ahead... Nothing. I looked to the right into the living room ... nothing. Then I looked left into the kitchen ...

I looked up on the top of the refrigerator. There, standing on 2 hind legs- a squirrel! Our eyes met momentarily- I screamed; he jumped, sliding across the kitchen countertop... leaping and scurrying across the dining table. Then, with a final leap, he was air born landing in a hanging plant. As the first plant swung, holding the squirrel within, additional carefully executed trapeze maneuvers to each successive pot was completed. Potting soil fell on the cream-colored carpets. I stood in amazement. It was like the best miniature circus I had ever seen.

I told Max to sit on the stairs and tap his cane to herd the critter towards the front door. After about 90 minutes, Mr. Squirrel made a beeline for freedom! Max enjoying all the excitement, said, "My wife's never gonna believe me when I tell her!"

I promptly replied, "Sure she will- just have her call me later." We laughed about the squirrel's antics and my questioning of his eyesight. And then I said, "I'll never doubt you again."

And my beloved, Elsie. Elsie was a wonderful, 93-year-old that had been married three times. Her stroke had left her debilitated with speech difficulties.

When I asked her about why she never updated her hearing aid, glasses and dentures, she replied, "Well," she said, "Several years ago, I had a heart attack. The doctors didn't expect me to live. So, I decided that I would give my farm to my son."

"But, then what happened", I asked.

"Well, you know… I got better and came home to this house, here". "And, then there was the next time when I got real sick again, and the doctors were sure that I wouldn't make it, so, I gave my son my boat and a couple of bank accounts. But, you know, I did get better."

"Last September, my doctors gave up on me again. For sure, I wouldn't make it; so, I gave my son the rest of my money and my car. And, wouldn't you know it? … again, I survived."

"So, Elsie", I asked, "Why don't you ask your son to give you those things you need?"

"Well, I don't really want to ask", she said softly.

I said, "If you can't ask him, I will".

A week later, Elsie called. She said, "You know what? I have an appointment for a new hearing aid. And, you know what else? I'm getting an eye exam. I even think that my son has made me a dentist appointment."

Days later, another call came. "This is the best; I can talk and hear you on the phone. And, my glasses will arrive next week. I'm like the bionic woman- I'm all new again!", Elsie remarked.

Elsie returned to her routine by walking to see her flowers blooming by the pond. She even painted her porch furniture. We remained close friends for years.

Wow! A year of highlights and they all taught me it was about how you touch others' lives. My success definition became the 4 C's: curiosity, compassion, comedy, and care: 1) Remaining curious about everything; 2) Viewing everyone through a compassionate lens; 3) Finding humor in every moment, and 4) Fondly caring by making personal connections.

I realized we all want success. Knowing what yours should be is key. I had stopped frustrating myself by living up to other's standards. By re-defining success, the 4 C's, I was doing my best every day, and helping others. So, yes, I was a success.

This fateful year came to an end. My reflections were over. I stopped worrying about other's definitions of success. I reflect on the 4 C's. Everything has become simpler. When you believe you are a success, you are.

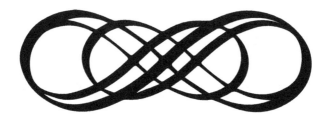

3

Shifting Sands in the Storm of Success

LENAE GOOLSBY JD.

About the Author:

In addition to her role as Practice Administrator for Infinite Health Integrative Medicine Center, LaNae is a Personal Power Activator, Public Speaker, Author & regularly featured expert as seen in Entrepreneur.com, MindBodyGreen.com, and others. Her mission is to help those who feel disempowered or victimized that they are in fact very much in power and capable of being the victor of their life experience, should they so choose to take their power back.

Website: www.LeNaeGoolsby.com

SHIFTING SANDS IN THE STORM OF SUCCESS

"Man's extremity is God's opportunity."
~ 2 Timothy 4:16-18

It was finally the end of another bleak and dreary day. The good news is that I survived the day and could plop down on the dirty cream velour sofa with a bottle of twelve-dollar Chardonnay. In pure exhaustion, a cloud of bleak depression, stress sufficient to break my back, fear, and let's not forget anger bordering on pure unadulterated rage, I reached for the television remote control.

"Revenge," an ABC Network show was on the television. This show was one of the bubblegum shows that I made a modicum of effort to watch weekly. I sat there, eyes glued to this superficial show like a mindless disciple, trying to numb my pain with the wine and mindless TV for at least the next hour.

On this particular mind-numbing event, I actually somehow managed to have an epiphany. It suddenly occurred to me that I was not watching "Revenge" for entertainment purposes. Rather, I was using this intellectually-challenging night time soap opera to fuel my anger and my own revenge ideations.

I used to tell people that I was *derailed* from pursuing practice through a series of cataclysmic events. But I now understand that life doesn't happen to me, life happens for me. And the life that is happening for me does so because consciously, or unconsciously, as the case may be, I create it. But, I did not realize this in 2011.

My husband's medical practice, our family's livelihood, was devastatingly impaled, like a torpedo through the heart, by local and national medical politics, as well as the crisis in pharmaceutical costs and acquisitions, and the ever-deepening Medicare cuts to physician reimbursement. Almost overnight we found ourselves hundreds of thousands of dollars in debt, unable to meet our personal financial obligations much less afford the chemotherapy drugs needed to continue providing cancer care to our patients.

My world, my security, if you will, went upside down eight days before Christmas in 2011. Emotionally I quickly escalated from shock, to depression, to anger. In my anger, I identified a couple of individuals as the malevolent culprits "responsible" for my family's financial crisis. Mentally I became fixated on getting back at the people who I believed threatened my marriage, ruined my financial security and peace of mind, and robbed me of my joy.

One evening, during this "storm" in my life, as I was working on a bottle of Chardonnay, and watching the ABC show, *Revenge*, I realized that I was not watching the show for entertainment, but rather for inspiration. It was in that moment that I realized that I could not continue to live in that state of mind anymore.

See, I at least knew enough at that point to know that when one goes out to dig a ditch for another person, they need to dig two graves because we cannot take someone else down without also taking ourselves down – thank you Confucius.

I mean, I really loathed and despised those hateful people for what they did to me and my family, but not enough to hurt myself in the process – at least not any more than I was already hurting. Besides, despite my fine and upstanding legal education, I could not figure out a karmic loophole. So, I turned off the TV and never watched Revenge again.

What I did do, however, is a complete 180-degree turnaround. I began a spiritual pursuit that led me to a quote popularized by Dr. Wayne Dyer that resonated like an epiphany for me: *"We are not physical beings having a spiritual experience; we are spiritual beings having a physical experience."*

I mean, I've kind of been taught that conceptual idea in church as a kid, but it never really resonated with me the way it did now. Think about it.

If we are infinite spiritual beings having a physical experience, then this dramatic and traumatic physical experience is, in the scheme of everything, nothing. A blip on the screen, a minor hiccup, a pebble in my shoe, easily removed with the right tools.

Over time, my perspective on all of my past experiences shifted and clarity, inner peace, and forgiveness replaced depression, stress, anger, and that unhinged desire for revenge.

While it was not easy or joyful by any means, our practice survived 2011 and 2012. And, at the end of 2013, we successfully transitioned The Oncology & Hematology Institute of Southwest Louisiana into what is known today as Infinite Health Integrative Medicine Center.

This new venture provides empowering motivational medicine for the body, mind & soul via our proprietary Four Pillar Approach to optimized health and longevity. Today, men and women, from all over the globe, who are ready for more than what traditional reactive medicine has to offer, seek Infinite Health out. Our patient-partners are achieving amazing transformational results, and we are impacting lives that would have never otherwise been reached had we not gone through the fire, so to speak.

In my limited, revenge-fueled spiral, I could have never conceived how that devastating day in 2011 could be the catalytic change required for the thriving, actually fun, and life-empowering medical practice we have today.

While continuing to fulfill my role as Practice Administrator for Infinite Health, I began my intuitive empowerment practice in 2013, after completing training in a universal laws-based spiritual and life-coaching program, and thereafter honed my intuitive abilities.

As an intuitive empowerment soul coach, I have the joy of helping my clients realize that they too are the creators of their life experience. We move from subconscious self-sabotage to become deliberate intenders and conscious creators. We work together to identify areas where our power has been abdicated and then we reclaim it. We observe what no longer serves and clear it in order to create the space for that which brings us closer to alignment with our bliss.

It is vital to the success of any endeavor, to be open and willing to shifting our sails, even if it means doing so in the middle of the storm.

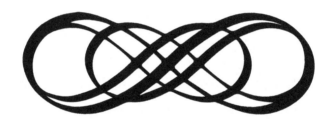

4

Finding My Spatula

LAURIE MEHRIN:

About the Author:

Laurie Mehring lives in Brooklyn, NY with her son Thomas and Wally and Bennie, who appear to be dogs. She grew up with severe sensory dysfunction and struggled for decades with perception, communication, and motor function, trying multiple different therapies, some successful and others not. She was diagnosed with moderate autism at age 39. This is her story of becoming employable; she works now as a visiting nurse.

Website: www.joyouslifewithautism.net

FINDING MY SPATULA

The strands of my thoughts slid over each other like spaghetti boiling in a pot. I could see a fiber of the conversation I wanted to have, but I couldn't find its ends; it was impossible to organize the words. As a young woman with undiagnosed autism, the outside world, as well as my jumbled brain, were incomprehensible.

Conversation required every bit of energy I could muster. I couldn't listen while another person spoke and at the same time think of what to say next. To me, "conversation" meant "I talk while you wait, and then you talk while I wait." I needed to plan my words in advance or else when I opened my mouth nothing would come out. When it was my turn I had to put pedal to the metal to send the words flying out in a rush, before they solidified into a hot, tarry ball behind my teeth. There was rarely any cohesion between what the other person said and what I replied. Sometimes, I said random things just to keep up the appearance that I was paying attention.

As a child, words and people were part of a chaotic wind that swirled around me. The words I heard spoken did not seem to describe what I saw, so I didn't bring them inside. While I could respond to a simple, direct request and comply with the rules, I made no attempt to generalize and apply those rules to similar situations. I was like a driver reacting to traffic lights and road signs without analyzing or remembering the instructions. No one gets out of the car and remembers the "conversation" with traffic.

I had no idea how to make new friends. During school dismissal, when kids waited for the buses, I walked over to a randomly chosen group of girls and tried to stand in their circle. I didn't say "Hello." I had no particular desire to speak to anyone in the group. I just tried to wedge myself in and get some idea of what they were talking about.

First, a girl to my right spoke, and then one to my left. Another in front of me said something, too. Conversation flowed over me in waves; individual words reached me, but never seemed to form any pattern, let alone a sentence. Words collided like opposing armies and were splayed across my consciousness with all the delicacy of urban warfare. Grammar was shot out of a Kalashnikov, a verb invaded my eye, and an adverb strafed my hair. I tried to participate, but my timing was off. I always seemed to say the wrong thing, at the wrong time. When the other girls laughed, I stared at the floor. When they were talking intently, I let out a twitter. They did not appreciate the intrusion and chased me off.

Despite my difficulties, I was determined to find my place in this world.

As a teenager I had a series of crap jobs in an effort to support myself. These did not go well. I not only did not deal well with other people, but I also became aware that my body and brain did not work together the way other people did.

I started off each job with the best intentions: I was going to listen to the boss and do what I was told.

But first I had to figure out what I was supposed to do, and that was hard! On my first day, there was always someone to show me how to do my job. Sometimes he was very patient, but no matter how slowly he spoke, I felt as if I were standing under a waterfall. Words gushed down on my head – important words that I needed to understand – but I couldn't catch enough of just the right drops. Instead, I had to shield myself against the torrent of words while, at the same time, work to understand what the person was saying. I stood under the cascade with my hands covering my head, my neck braced. Trying not to panic, my ears raced to process the data, but more kept coming. I couldn't slow the flow, so to stop the words from hitting me, I deflected them into a pile. I couldn't push them too far away; they had to be within my reach so I could retrieve them later, when I was alone and it was safe to think. Then, I gathered up the words and tried to bring them home and examine them under a microscope. I was exhausted before my first

lunch break.

I had a few warehouse jobs and wondered why my fingers did not move as quickly as the girls I worked with. I couldn't coordinate reading the packing list, finding the desired item, going to where that item was on the shelf, taking it off the shelf, and placing it in a box. My feet moved slowly, my body refused to turn, and my hands would not grab. I thought there was a problem with my hands, like poor manual dexterity. Now I understand that to perform a task, I need to give my individual body parts specific instructions about what each is supposed to do. The sequence of movements has to be carefully enunciated, and each step completed before I could move on to the next one. A pick-and-pack line is no place for contemplation, so I did not last long.

"What is wrong with me?" I wondered. "Why am I so much worse than everyone else that I can't even perform a simple job?" Determined as always, I set out the next day with the fortitude of a hiker on the

Appalachian Trail — laden with gear, aware of the sun's position in the sky, and knowing that following a seemingly never-ending series of rocks and trees would lead me somewhere; I just had to keep walking.

In college I took literature and writing classes and began pursuing a degree in English. I wasn't sure what I would do if I actually caught an English degree, but I pursued it, anyway.

In one of my writing classes, we had only one assignment for the whole semester: to tell our own story. That class was my first experience of working with other writers, sharing what we experienced in one another's work and how it made us feel. It was easy for me to write about anything and to allow another person to read it. Things that would have been impossible for me to speak flowed freely from my pen. Even when I read my own words in front of a group, I felt enough distance to grease the words' passage through my throat.

The physical act of producing speech was never a problem for me; my downfall had always been facing another person without having a speech already written. Whenever I looked at someone and tried to think of something to say, I felt as if a pile of words were sitting on the floor of my brain but I didn't know how to string them together to form a sentence. It was like staring into my cupboard wondering how to turn some of the cans and dried things into a meal. Writing class became my cookbook; pen and paper were my pot and spatula.

I worked as a home health aide for several years, and was reasonably competent at it, so in 1990 I decided to give nursing school a try. With my previous experience, the first semester went well. During my second semester of school, the clinical work became more difficult. A hospital is a very busy place, and I was plagued both by my susceptibility to overstimulation and my inability to process what was said to me in real time.

On the first day of the week, I met my assigned patient, helped him bathe and exercise, administered his meds, and provided whatever other assistance he needed. I documented in his chart and read the other notes. Altogether, this took about four hours. By the following day, I was expected to have researched the patient's condition and be prepared to give a report to the group on his disease and the recommended treatment. All this I could handle.

The problem arose when the instructor wanted to observe my work. I couldn't listen to her comments and work at the same time. Alone with the patient, I could focus on the visual task. Making small talk with him while I fetched a basin of water did not distract me. I knew that the instructor was only trying to help me become a better nurse and that her comments were well intentioned. Had I understood my disability, I would have stopped what I was doing, and focused only on the instructor. When I tried to listen while performing my patient-care tasks, I became overwhelmed and lost awareness of my hands and feet. I could very easily find myself standing in the middle of the patient's room with a full washbasin in my hands and not know what I was supposed to do next.

With persistence, supportive friends, faith in God, and the help of a variety of professionals I managed to find the boulders and shallow places in the river and made it across. I became a registered nurse in 1994.

The grace I was given was the ability to listen. Beginning my first job in a nursing home, I learned to turn off my aural filters and hear what the person was saying as if it were a song. Instead of trying to understand each individual word, I listened to the rhythm and pattern of the music. Slowly, it began to make sense.

In the past, words had been an impediment. They fell on my head like a waterfall, and I had to stop them from hitting me. Now I let the cascade flow over me, as if I were standing in a warm summer rain. I didn't need to analyze each drop – only allow the overall pattern to soak me with its meaning.

So, when my supervisor explained the job to me, I simply listened and did not try to understand each word. Then I watched what the other nurses did and read the materials I was given. Through repetition and practice, I began to absorb and learn.

If I had understood my disability, I would not have become a nurse, because so much of what nurses do is multitasking. In a hospital, all of the patients, plus the doctors and other staff, are screaming for the nurse at the same time. Fortunately,

I have managed to find jobs where my tasks are sequential. I have worked in home care for the last 20 years. I only have one patient at a time, so I can work at my own pace, taking time to process my thoughts. I have to expect to get interrupted, but it can only be one disturbance at a time, since I only have one phone on which to receive incoming calls. It gives a cautious thoughtfulness to my work, which the elderly seems to appreciate.

Single tasking, listening to the music in speech, and cooking up some yummy paragraphs, I wade into this river that is my life. The water flows around me, guides me, buoys me, and nourishes me.

5

LaVue Boutique

RAYMA GARRAWAY:

About the Author:

Rayma Garraway is the co-founder and owner of LaVue Boutique, an apart-rent vacation community on the island of Anguilla. LaVue received 4.5 stars on Trip Advisor and gets high marks for hospitality and beautiful views. Rayma became interested in Real Estate as a vehicle for creating wealth early in her life and earned her real estate license at a young age.

She understands that no one becomes successful by themselves and is grateful for all of the people who helped her on her journey. This is why she believes in the axiom of "pay it forward" and mentors' women of color to become independent and successful people in business and life.

Through her not for profit organization Never Happier, Inc., Rayma teaches others the skills necessary to excel at life and be in service to others. Never Happier has helped (need numbers) people manifest lives they could only imagine. Rayma is also the President of the Brooklyn chapter of the Health & Wellness Network of Commerce, a community of heart-centric entrepreneurs dedicated to improving the lives of others.

She lives a life of travel and fine food with her new hubby.

Website: http://lavueanguilla.com/

LaVue Boutique

I am sitting at my mom's desktop computer. I can feel a smile on my lips. It's strange because I haven't smiled in a long time. I am reading through my email and opened an attachment. I am looking at an executed contract. It is staring me dead in the face. After years of back and forth, countless meetings and so many dinners I am a co-owner of a boutique resort on the island of Anguilla. This is amazing. I am so very happy that words can't describe it. Two weeks later I used this as motivation to raise capital from potential investors for another resort. After a few days my bank statement showed $120,000 of investor's money with a twelve-month term to pay; with another $80,000 out in the field waiting for a sale of about $150,000. Life is but a dream. What more can one ask for at my age?

Residual income, that's what that deal gave me. A lifetime of paychecks. Don't get me wrong, there's nothing wrong with a onetime check of $500, or $5,000 or even $50,000. A check without restrictions of how it can be used is great, but that thing called residual income - somebody help me! Seeing your dreams come true after so many years of hard work is an incredible satisfying feeling. When it happens to you, my friend, you will be on Cloud Nine.

You may ask how I got here. You want the truth? I'll give you the truth, the whole truth, and nothing but the truth. It was prayer. Or favor. It was being at the right place at the right time.I realized early on that I had a great love for travel and food. For two years I have been work-vacationing on the same island. There's something magical about it. The turquoise sea water, the perfect white powdery sand; and if you want something coarser we could head over to the east side of the island and find a rougher grade of pink sand. As I write this, I can feel chills running through my body.

There is very little to do on my island. They have the most amazing beaches and the sweetest lobster I ever tasted. I am a big foodie and have made it my ritual that once I am on the island, every Sunday lunch is on a private Cay that is just three minutes off the mainland. I would love to take you there with me one day. You could be my travel buddy.

My host, who later became my boyfriend, and I were sitting on the beach. With my foot in the sand, I was gazing into the ocean. The smell of the salt is refreshing and the sound of the waves hitting the shore is quite relaxing. My attention is taken away from the lapping waves by a side conversation I hear about the island. People are saying it is in shit. *Huh, in shit?* I zoned in. I was all eyes and ears. I learned to observe and pay attention by watching the Jews take over East New York, Brooklyn until they made their way to Bushwick. Their success was credited to seeing opportunity through people's struggles.

If you want gossip go to a bar or a barbershop. The best and the worst news - you'll find it out there. But take it with a grain of salt because there are a lot of stories that must be filtered out. I am listening to two men in conversation. The more they drink the louder they talk, and this is good for me. One man is saying how the government isn't doing anything for the country. The other man replies that the banks are in turmoil.

If the banks are in turmoil that can only mean people aren't paying their loans.

A plan began to form in my mind. In order to be successful you must quit talking and begin doing. The following morning, I went to all banks on the island and requested their foreclosure lists. Some lists I was able to walk out of the bank with and others I had to set up appointments to see.

Unfortunately, I only had three more days left on the island, so I did as much research I could during those three remaining days.

Upon landing back in New York City, I immediately booked a ticket to return to the island. This trip wasn't for fun. I had a mission.

While in New York, I continued my research and decided on which properties I wanted to visit. Six weeks later and with a list of specific properties, I once again stepped onto the sandy beaches of the island and set about searching for the ones I targeted. If anyone has ever visited the Caribbean, you know that there are rarely house numbers. You have to depend on asking people walking the streets or sitting under a mango tree how to get to where you are going.

The road was surrounded on both sides by overgrowth. Road maybe too strong a word. It was really a path of sea rocks. My car bounced around as I drove. *Oh my God, what happens if my tire pops!* After a few miles the jungle opened up to a beautiful ocean view. The LaVue Hotel was a three-story pale-yellow inn with balconies that overlooked the island. It sat in the middle of the island away from other hotels and resorts. It was gorgeous.

LaVue was owned by a husband and wife. The husband was bald with beautiful hazel eyes and dressed in a blue tee tucked into his jeans and sandals. The wife was strong and fit but tired. She looked miserable.

Two things struck me about the hotel. One, up close you could see it needed work. Chipped painted, small cracks, and while it had two pools they were both missing tiles and there were leaves floating on the surface. And two, each room was built with natural rock and was unique.

I spoke with the husband and wife for about two hours. I was already seeing the renovation in my mind. Along with a name change - LaVue Boutique Inn.

The following Sunday I returned to the bar and bought the guys a drink as a thank you for the lead. For a girl from Brooklyn, I couldn't believe I had achieved all this. After years of challenges and failures, it was good to finally smile.

6

FROM DEVASTATION TO RECOUPMENT AND BEYOND

ROBERT SHIELDS:

About the Author:

Robert Shields founded Piedmont Mining Company, Inc. in the early 1980s and has been its Chairman, President and Chief Executive Officer ever since. He has had a lifetime of experience in exploration and mining, especially for precious metals, and has also worked on Wall Street. In April 1985, Piedmont put into production the first operating gold mine in the eastern United States since 1942 at its Haile Gold Mine property in Lancaster County, South Carolina.

This gold deposit occurs in saprolitic and heavily altered rocks, and in a climate with considerable rainfall and occasional hurricanes. It was probably the first gold mine in the United States to use heap leach extraction technology in a wet humid environment with acid rock conditions. Piedmont operated the Haile Gold Mine for 6 years until 1992, when it entered into a joint venture with Amax Gold Inc. Piedmont also controlled ten other gold properties in North and South Carolina at that time. In addition to gold and silver, Piedmont was also engaged in exploration for heavy mineral sands deposits in eastern North Carolina, and it also operated a clay mine in South Carolina, producing white, fine grained clay which was sold to electronics and paint companies.

In 2003 Piedmont commenced exploration for gold and silver in the western United States, primarily in Nevada and Arizona, through option and earn in agreements with other junior exploration companies.

Mr. Shields has had experience with contract drillers, permitting, water and environmental matters and refineries and has 25 years of experience running a publicly traded company.

Mr. Shields was an associate with Morgan Stanley & Co. in corporate finance, primarily mergers and acquisitions, in the early 1970s and was a security analyst with Paine, Webber, Jackson and Curtis in the mid-1960s. He also worked briefly as a mining analyst in Sydney, Australia in 1970.

He has an extensive background in geology, mineralogy, geochemistry, nuclear chemistry, the origin and evolution of the earth, mineral deposits, exploration and mining. He graduated Cum Laude and with High Distinction in Geology from Dartmouth College in 1960. He then received a PhD degree in Geochemistry from the Massachusetts Institute of Technology in 1965, where he was elected to Sigma Xi, Honorary Scientific Society, and Phi Lambda Upsilon, Honorary Chemical Society. He also received an MBA from the Stanford University Graduate School of Business Administration in 1971.

He was an officer in the US Army Corps of Engineers from 1967 to 1969, where he spent two years at NASA working on the first Earth Resources Technology Satellite and was honorably discharged with the rank of Captain.

He is a member of the American Geophysical Union, the New York Academy of Sciences, the American Geological Institute, the Prospectors and Developers Association of Canada, the Society for Mining, Metallurgy and Exploration, Inc. and a new member of The Explorers Club.

Website: www.

FROM DEVASTATION TO RECOUPMENT AND BEYOND

Easter is a lovely time of year and Easter Sunday is one of those special days when my dear wife likes to go to Church. It was Easter Sunday morning, April 5, 2015. Margaret poked me and told me to get out of bed. We can't miss the Easter Sunday service. We got ready and left for Church, only 2 blocks from our apartment. We were approaching the steps into Church. Margaret leaned up against the Church wall. She hesitated for a moment and then dropped to the sidewalk at my feet! Yikes! I thought she had fainted. But then I noticed she was gasping for air. Within a few minutes two ambulances arrived.

They told me to step aside as they tended to her. They picked her up, put her into one of the ambulances and told me to get into the other one. We sped with sirens blaring to the Presbyterian Hospital 6 blocks away. When I got there they were carrying her into the emergency room while pumping at her chest.

They led me into a small room near where Margaret was being treated. They already had 8 doctors working on her. I was getting worried. A few minutes later someone came in and told me they were going to give it one more try. Yikes! Now I was scared. Then reality set in - there was no hope. She was gone! Impossible, I thought. One hour before we had been walking into Church and now she was dead?? How could that be?

They took me into a small room where Margaret lay and told me I could stay as long as I wished. There was my beautiful wife with a large plastic tube sticking out of her throat! I held her hand, only it was cold because she was DEAD! I started crying uncontrollably. I looked up and Jennifer, the Rector of our Church, was standing beside us. I just kept crying. Jennifer said some prayers for us, but I couldn't stop crying. We had been happily married for 38 years and suddenly she was gone. I would never see her again in this life. She was 8 years younger than I. How could she have died before me??

I stayed with her for several hours, just crying and crying. Finally, mid-afternoon, my good friend, Seth, led me back to our apartment. It was then that it really sank in that she would never again be with me. Everywhere I looked reminded me of Margaret: her desk, the decorations and paintings on our walls, her dresser with her lipsticks and hairbrushes, etc. I just kept crying. It was terrible.

A few days later, our two wonderful daughters, Jenny and Ginger, arrived to try to comfort me. We all cried together. It was too horrible to contemplate. Then there was the funeral. The Church was packed. Standing room only. I cried through the whole service. I was a mess.

Two weeks later I was having dinner with Ginger and Seth at a nearby restaurant. After we finished dinner we got up to leave, only I couldn't get up from the table. I tried again but couldn't arise. My left side wouldn't work! The waitresses thought I was drunk, but I emphasized that I was not drunk. There was something wrong with my left side. Ginger and Seth then helped me out of the restaurant and escorted me home.

I hobbled around our apartment for the next two days. Seth and Ginger then took me to Seth's doctor who told them to take me to Lenox Hill for an MRI. I was escorted into a room with some high-tech equipment in it and told to lay on my back, motionless as they fed me into a big machine head first. I must not move!

The MRI was successful. Seth's doctor then called and told him to take me to the emergency room at the Lenox Hill Hospital. I had had a stroke!

A stroke? I was healthy! No one in my family had ever had a stroke. Upon entering the emergency room the seriousness of my situation began to sink in. I was put on a bed and subjected to one test after another. For the next two days I was monitored constantly. The environment was terrifying. People were dying on both sides of me. Next of kin were runningup and down the halls screaming and crying. OMG. Am I going to die too? What is going to happen to me?

After two days Ginger told me that they had a bed for me at the Rusk Rehabilitation Center on 17th Street. I was loaded into a wheelchair and taken to the 12th floor where I was 'locked' into a very high-tech bed. A nurse pressed some buttons on my bed recording my weight, so should I touch the floor with one of my feet, an alarm would go off and nurses would come piling in. There was no escaping. Their motto was 'safety before privacy'. I could not even go to the bathroom by myself!!

Rehab was like boot camp. The day started at 5 am when you were awakened to monitor your vital signs. Then you

42

got an injection - in your stomach! At 7 am - breakfast, then therapy followed. After a while my stomach looked like a pincushion from all the needles that had been stuck into me. Every other day they wheeled me into a shower room, stripped me and hosed me down. It was like being run through a car wash.

I wondered if I would ever walk again. The physical therapy was tough, but the prospect of never walking again terrified me. What if I were confined to a wheelchair for the rest of my life? I kept at the therapy diligently. At the end of the third week, my physical therapist led me outside, around the block and down a set of subway stairs.

I passed! I could walk again without help. I wouldn't need a wheelchair. Several days later they discharged me. I was delivered to my apartment. I could once again function like a normal person. I missed my dear wife terribly but at least I was still alive and could walk.

At that point I realized I was on my own! I walked slowly and with difficulty, but at least I could walk. But I would have to do therapy by myself if I was to improve further. Grrrrr. To make matters worse, friends told me that the surviving spouse often dies within a year of the death of the first. I vowed that would NOT happen to me!

I started doing exercises. Lifting a 5-pound weight with my left arm. Then there were squats. After a few weeks I was doing 10, then 15. Most importantly, I was to walk 1 to 2 miles per day. That is tough for me. I have to think about every step I take. My walking has now recovered significantly.

In the meantime, I have started looking for new endeavors. I have become a Reader in Church. I walk to the front and pull myself up to the podium. I get many compliments when I read.

Then my Primary Doctor told me to find a girlfriend. Wow. At 79 years old I hadn't thought that possible. After a few months of searching diligently I have found a remarkable lady. I am so lucky! She inspires me to practice the piano and search out new endeavors. I have also recently been accepted for membership in the Explorers Club.

That is a great honor! And I have now given my first lecture on rocks and mi

7

AWAKEN - My Journey to Self-Love and Self-Acceptance

SAMANTHA CERVINO

About the Author:

Samantha Cervino P. is no stranger to change. In fact, her life has changed dramatically many times over - and she in turn has touched the lives of many on her fascinating journey. At age 14, she emigrated with her family from her native Uruguay leaving friends, traditions and everything she knew behind; For a new life in Toronto, Canada.

Just a few short years ago her life took another dramatic turn, leading her down a path of true purpose and fulfillment. As a global change maker and moderator for the Wellness Universe, Samantha has changed and improved the lives of many, including children with special needs as well as countless clients in her practice of energy healing.

In addition to being an accomplished leader in her field of understanding and shifting human emotions through Reiki and EFT, she is also a blogger, published author and motivates through her work on social media.

As a master energy healer, Samantha is committed to the personal success of her clients and is often quoted for saying "Life is to be felt, not planned."

Website: https://smbalternativehealing.me/

AWAKEN -MY JOURNEY TO SELF-LOVE AND SELF-ACCEPTANCE

Thirty-nine years of my life were spent looking for answers. I was exhausted, unhappy, empty, unfulfilled. But why? My life was complete, or so I thought. The feeling of loneliness and unhappiness occupied a big space in my heart. Being a mother was the only thing that fulfilled me. My son is the greatest gift God gave me. I made a promise to myself to be the best mother my son could ever have. I make it a priority to ensure he has everything he needs along with my full support.

But I desperately needed to have more of a purpose in life than being a mother and a wife. It was not enough. My soul was yearning for more. I faced many challenges and situations in my life. Often, I felt I was a victim, unlucky, limited to life's abundance, wondering why I did not have what others who seemed happy and wealthy had. I always wanted more and never stopped to appreciate what I already had. But I grew up like that, limited. A middle child with a severe middle child syndrome, there is such thing as a middle child syndrome, and I had it bad. Always feeling like an outsider and misunderstood in my own family!

When I was fourteen, my family moved from Uruguay to Canada. I had mixed feelings about the move, as this was a strange and confusing age for me. I left behind my best friend and my first childhood love; he was the only friend that accepted me with all my faults and never judged me. I survived this change and adapted well. I fell in love with

Canada and its people.

I got married young and my first marriage resulted in a bitter divorce, followed by many meaningless relationships, hurts, and disappointments. In my head, I was a victim, unlucky, doomed to be forever unhappy. I would look in the mirror and wonder why my life was such a mess asking myself repeatedly what I did to deserve this?

In my mid-twenties I met a man who, three years later would be my second husband. With him, I fell in love and had my first and only son. I thought I had it all and yet I still did not feel entirely complete, that empty void was still there. We moved a lot because of my husband's career. I left my family, friends and worked to support his work so we could have a better life, more wealth and the opportunity for me to stay home and raise our son. I was finally living the life the way I always wanted! So I thought.

My husband's career took him away from home a lot, and for a long time, I was alone and lonely in my marriage, in this life we had built for us. This loneliness resulted in sadness and depression, blaming my husband for my unhappiness. Years later and after three moves from Canada to the USA and from the USA back to Canada and seven years after the birth of our son I asked for a divorce. I was done.

I did not know who I was. Did not recognize myself. I was tired of being unhappy and feeling unloved. Am I not lovable, I asked? Am I not enough? From childhood, I carried a lot of limiting beliefs. I was convinced I was not meant to be happy. I was blaming the world for my misfortune. I was in a very low energy frequency hence attracting people and circumstances of a lower vibration.

At the age of thirty-nine, I made myself a promise, that my forties would be the best years of my life! Separated from my husband I embarked on my journey to self-love and self-acceptance. Desperate to find some answers and committed to my promise to live happily ever after.

I met a friend who is an energy healer and had a few Bio Energy sessions with her. I was ready to try anything. To my pleasant surprise, I started to feel more balanced, clear headed, and grounded. My energy began to shift from negative to positive, from heavy to light and I felt rejuvenated! I also had the opportunity to receive Reiki healing, and I fell in love with this practice so much so that I became a Reiki Master. I used Reiki to heal myself, to heal my soul.

I no longer blame the world for my past misfortunes but instead, have great understanding and acceptance for all my past experiences with people and circumstances. I had to change some things in my life and distance myself from certain acquaintances and friends. I had to "clean up" to fulfill my life's purpose.

Today, I can say that Reiki saved my life. Energy healing brought me back to life. It taught me self-love, self-respect, self-acceptance, self-esteem, courage. I am making my forties the best years of my life! Just like I promised I would. I feel fantastic, full of love and life. I affirm I am lovable; I am abundant, I am grateful, I am motivated, I am deserving of all the Universe has to offer…and so are YOU! I am here to tell you that the greatest gift you can give yourself is self-love.

When we love ourselves first, then we can love others. When we like who we are, we are never lonely. I had a paradigm shift. I have gratitude in my heart for every single thing and person in my life. I love my self and humanity. I learned we are all the same, made by the same creator yet unique in our own way. We are all here to make this world even more beautiful than it already is.

Patti,
Thank you for all of your love and support over the years. I wish you the best of everything in life
love Todd

8

I AWAKEN AS I SLEEP

TODD LE BOUEF:

About the Author:

Todd is the Founder/Owner of Mi[...]
& Beyond near Oswego, NY. As a [...]
Clairsentient, Clairvoyant, Clairaud[...]
and Writer, Todd is dedicated to guid[...]
Spiritual Path.

Website: www.mbsr61.com

I Awaken as I Sleep

"As you sow in your subconscious mind, so shall you reap in your body and environment."

~ Joseph Murphy, The Power of Your Subconscious Mind

For those of us who do energy work such as Reiki, it is not about us. We are the conduit of the energy flowing through us to help our client reduce their stress so their body can heal on its own. In my experience, no two sessions are ever the same. Being a Reiki Master Teacher of four years and an Intuitive Empath, I sometimes see colors, images and visions. Even spirits can show up in a session. However, I have never had the profound experience I am about to share with you happen to me before.

In the Spring of 2016 I received a text from my long time dear friend Mary, asking if I would send distance Reiki to her nephew Tim. I asked what the nature of the problem was. Mary texted, "Tim overdosed on drugs and he is in ICU in a medically-induced coma". As I read this I recalled many memories of Tim. I had known him since he was 3 years old. At this point and time, Tim was 24 years of age. Mary and Colleen were ex sisters-in-law but they both were, and still are, mothers to Tim. We all were and still are great friends to this day.

Tim was a vivacious child growing up, with a very creative imagination. Both of his "moms" gave him the guidance and tools he needed in life. Tim went through different stages like most kids do. For example, he explored a serious Goth stage, and he did it very well, not caring what others thought of him. So imagine the contrast of getting this news and having a flood of great memories run through your mind.

That very afternoon I arrived at the hospital ICU waiting room. Tim's family was all there greeting me and exchanging hugs. As I sat with Colleen, she explained to me that he would be in this induced coma for at least a week. Tim's body was detoxing, going through withdrawal and as a result he became very agitated. Putting him in this coma state would allow his body to heal faster. I offered to do a Reiki session on Tim and Colleen agreed. We went into his room where he was hooked up to IV lines pumping various medicines into his system.

Not only were there nurses in his room, but this hospital is very conservative about alternative modalities, so I had to be discreet. I sat next to Tim's bed and laid my hand on his arm, starting my intention of the Reiki energy flowing through his body. As I was doing this I could feel muscle movement in his arm, so I knew he knew I was there, and he was responding to this energy.

I went back the next day to do another session on Tim, only this time I had the room to myself. I was able to be less discreet in administering Reiki. I remember being at the end of Tim's bed, laying my hands on his ankles. I closed my eyes and set my intention to let the Reiki energy flow up through his legs and throughout his body, out through the crown of his head, pushing out any harmful toxins.

Right at that moment I heard Tim's voice speaking to me. "I am sorry about what I did. I am not really sure why I did this. I didn't mean to upset my family and friends. I don't want them to be upset or disappointed in me." As I heard this I remember saying to myself, "Whoa! Did this really just happen?" I realized that Tim and I had connected in his subconscious mind.

I replied to Tim, "Tim, at this very moment it doesn't matter why you did this. You realize what you did was not optimal. Just learn from this experience. When you know better, you'll do better. No one is upset or disappointed in you. We would like you to come back to us, so we can support and help you in any way we can. We love you!" Tim said thank you and the conversation ended. I closed the session with an affirmation and stood quietly for a moment.

At that point, my spirit guide said to share a message with his Mom that this was meant to happen.

"Tim was to experience this to help him 'awaken' and to have a different perspective on his life. It was not his time to leave. He is on this Earth to help others. This is part of his soul's blueprint. Look at this as a positive experience for Tim. Wait, and things will unfold in time."

Now remember, Tim was supposed to be in a coma for at least a week. After having this subconscious conversation, Tim's condition improved immensely. The doctors were amazed at how well he was doing after only three days, so they decided to take him out of the coma. Tim's continued improvement allowed his release from the hospital two days later. He then went to a Mental Health facility for a week of counseling.

To quote Dr. Jill Carnahan, "Your subconscious mind controls all the vital processes of your body. It already knows the answers to your problems and it already knows how to heal you."

Even in Tim's subconscious mind, he was fearful that what he had done might cause backlash from his loved ones. This fear was blocking his ability to heal. Tim's subconscious knew the answers; it knew that having this conversation was necessary to put his fears to rest, allowing him to heal quicker.

It never ceases to amaze me what can happen in Reiki sessions. This success is not due to me, but being open to the power of intention and energy work, even in the subconscious mind. Tim acknowledges that he has some vague sense of the subconscious conversation that took place. That in of itself is pretty powerful!

It has been over a year since this incident happened and Tim is doing great. He has made it a point to connect with nature on a regular basis to let go of the everyday stresses and demands of his life. This allows him time to recharge his internal human batteries, helping him stay aligned and at peace within himself.

To maintain peace within, it is important to be open to spending time in nature. The overstimulation of technology and other people's energies needs to be wiped clean. There is no Wi-Fi in nature but I promise you will find a better connection. This is a healthy way to help you live a happy, peaceful life.

"Nature does not hurry, yet everything is accomplished" ~ *Tao Tzu*

9
THE SPOON

DR. PAT BARRINGTON:

About the Author:

Dr. Patricia Barrington has been a Speaker and a Women Empowerment Coach for over 17 years. She is also a New York City retired Public School teacher. She conducts conferences in the United States, Africa, and the Caribbean. She is the author of Breaking Generational Chains: A Woman's Guide to Freedom. Dr.  Barrington's mission is to and help one million women live a life of Victory, Influence, and Power, so they can pass it on to the next generation.

Website: www.drpatriciabarrington.com

THE SPOON

I looked down. Blood was dripping down from my hand. The rinse from the shower was washing it down the drain.

Moments before, my mother had broken into the bathroom, a metal spoon lifted high above her. She drew back the shower curtain and began to hit me mercilessly. Tears flowed down my checks as I held up my hands to block the attack - and just like that, my finger split open.

I was so angry. I felt like hitting her back. It took everything I had not to. I reached out and gripped on to the spoon as tightly as I could. As my grip got tighter, I danced around so I could position myself directly in front of the door of the bathroom. I let go of the spoon and ran as fast as I could into my bedroom, slamming the door shut and quickly locking it behind me.

I started to get dressed for work; while my mother was on the other side of door yelling at me.

How did we get here, you ask?

Good question. The answer dealt with my cousin LaFleur.

LaFleur came to live with us from the Caribbean and everything was going well. One day, she asked me about my friend, Jen. She wanted to know what the story was with Jen. Her questions sounded a lot like accusations. She demanded to know what "went down."

I told her my story.

Jen was my friend while I lived in St. Vincent. We went to the same Church and attended Youth Meetings every week. She came to New York two years after I arrived and was staying with her oldest brother and his family. She was experiencing some difficulties with her sister in law.

Jen and I went to the movies in Times Square and then walked around looking at all the bright lights and the massive number of people. I told her that she could stay with me if she needed to get away.

The next day, I let my mother know Jen was coming over to spend the weekend.

"No! not in my apartment!"

I was confused. *Why couldn't Jen stay here? Was it because Jen's sister in law and my mother were close?* I stood my ground. "I pay rent here too, and what is going on with Jen and your friend have nothing to do with me."

My mother walked away.

LaFleur went and told my mother what I said, or her version of what I said. My mother became furious and vindictive towards me. She told me that I could not use the cookware and utensils in her kitchen. I couldn't afford to buy my own cookware. I was paid minimum wage and living paycheck to paycheck. I got paid twice a month and if there were three weekends before my pay date, I had to borrow money for my subway fare to get to work. I paid for rent, gas, electricity, my subway to school and work and I brought home less than $400.00 bi-weekly. *How* was I going to cook and eat?

The situation between my mother and myself quickly went from bad to worse.

One evening my mother went to a meeting. LaFleur stayed home and her sister came over to visit. I was walking down the hallway, going to my bedroom with my $2.50 Chicken Fried Rice from the take-out Chinese joint and looked towards my mother's bedroom. They both were sitting on the floor eating the biggest plate of rice and peas, with vegetables: cabbage, carrots and string beans, and roast chicken. They had a tall glass on pineapple juice on the dresser as they laughed and ridiculously gorged their faces with expensive food.

LaFleur saw me, and then her sister looked in my direction. They seemed nervous.

I locked my gaze on the sisters and stepped into my mother's bedroom. I looked down at my simple chicken fried rice in its Styrofoam tray. It was all I could afford after bills and taxes were paid to la Casa de Mama.

I had had enough. I was sick of their condescending chuckles. I walked into the bedroom

"Get out now!" *How dare they get to have Sunday Dinner in my house and I am not able to even make a cup of tea.*

"We are not leaving because your mother says we can spend the evening here."

"She is not here now, so you need to go."

They refused to leave. I walked to the dresser, took one of the glasses of juice and poured it over my cousin's head.

When my mother came back that evening LaFleur told her what happened. My mother came looking for me to show me who was boss. I locked myself in my bedroom and did not open the door.

"Open this door!"

"Call me on the phone," I replied. I knew she wanted to throw her authority around and shame me in front of my two cousins, and I refused to let her.

She waited until the next morning while I was taking a shower. And now, we are back to where we started - The infamous spoon incident.

In retrospect, it's funny. Getting hit with a spoon is a story many minorities share around the table as we compare war stories; but in reality, it's not at all a joke.

We need to do something about how we connect and relate to our children, so we don't get violent and out of control, regardless of what is going on in our own heart and life; or what we bring with us from our past.

And because of that, I want to stop the emotional abuse and empower Moms to create a safe haven for their children, leaving a legacy of love and peace.

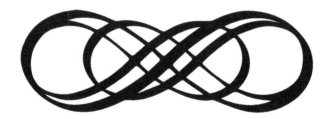

10

HOW I LEARNED TO SERVE NOT SELL

GARY H KARP:

About the Author:

Gary is a brand and marketing strategist. He supports authors, coaches, and small businesses develop a online identity by creating a comprehensive marketing strategy allowing them to generate more leads, sell more products and services, and bring more value to the world. He cut his teeth in the world of Marketing Research, working with such agencies as Young & Rubicam, Ogilvy & Mather, and Saatchi & Saatchi. Today he works with small companies such as Dragon Phoenix Media, TechnoFear Productions, and Nightforce International helping them grow their communities and spread their message.

Schedule your free 30-minute strategy session with Gary by visiting: http://bit.ly/FREEstrategysessionwithGary

Website: www.garyhkarp.com

How I learned to Serve not Sell

For most of my professional life I have been in sales and marketing in one-way shape or form. I have worked retention for America Online and customer service for AT&T Mobility and Optimum; a little note, Customer Service is just another way of saying sales since every representative is required to up-sell products and services at least two times on every call. I have sold Life Insurance and Financial Services for Banker's Life and Casualty and Aflac. I have sold electronics and jewelry for numerous retailers.

All my training was centered around hard sells and the concept of "ABC" (Always Be Closing). I learned multiple closing techniques like the Lincoln Close, the Assumptive Close, and the A/B Close.

And I was good at it. When I decided to strike out on my own in 2014 and start my own consulting business, I networked and met prospects the only way I knew how. Direct, salesy, and using manipulative closing techniques. I was always focusing on me - my skills, my accomplishments, my training - instead of focusing on the prospect and what they needed. I believed that putting forth the benefits of what I do and my expertise BEFORE discovering what challenges others were facing was the way to be successful. Tell them what they need. Don't ask.

While I got a few clients here and there, my business was not growing to a sustainable level. I decided to hire a coach to help me. It was then I was introduced to Relationship Marketing. Relationship Marketing is built on the principles of KLT; people do business with people they Know, Like, and Trust.

That should have been my A-HA moment, but it wasn't.

I took the advice from my coach, but only at the surface level. I asked all the right questions, feigned interest in people, and made a few suggestions while holding my gold nuggets hostage until they forked over their credit card. I was still focusing on how people could help me and how much money I could extract from them.

People can sense insincerity a mile away. While I thought I was being clever, I was really slipping on the loud plaid sports jacket of a used car salesman. I didn't land any new business and my old business was drying up. *This crap doesn't work!*

I doubled down on sales techniques and manipulation, but still nothing changed. Then a friend gave me a copy of Steven Covey's Seven Habits of Highly Effective People. In it, he uses the metaphor of an Emotional Bank Account to build trust and rapport with people and describes how to make deposits. I also remembered the famous quote from Zig Ziglar, "You can have everything you want in life if you only help enough other people get what they want first."

Out of desperation I decided too commit myself to these philosophies and see what happened. I started to approach every meeting with others as an opportunity to serve and gave freely of myself without expectation of anything in return. I left it all on the table and took genuine interest in other people's challenges and offered practical, actionable solutions. I did this everywhere. Networking events, in my Facebook Groups, standing in line at the grocer. I took every opportunity to serve and contribute.

At first nothing changed. I began to think my original thought that people were nothing more than leeches who took and took while providing no value in return was true. I pushed that thought out of my head and continued to believe in serving and contribution.

It started slowly. One gentleman I gave advice to on starting a podcast reached out and asked me to coach him on the process. A women I shared strategies with on how to grow her vocal coaching business left a beautiful recommendation for me without being asked to do so. A doctor offered a trade in services after I helped him design a plan to get more clients. Please note that none of these people were my clients when I gave them my support. They were just people I met in my day to day life.

Now I lead with the concept of "ABV" (Always Bring Value) instead of ABC. My business is starting to grow and become sustainable. More importantly, I have made friends and trusted business associates by making deposits in their Emotional Bank Accounts.

I may not always get the client by doing business this way, but I always live congruently with my beliefs and provide value at every turn.

If you would like to schedule a FREE strategy session with me and see how I may serve and support you, you may do so by visiting http://bit.ly/FREEstrategysessionwithGary.

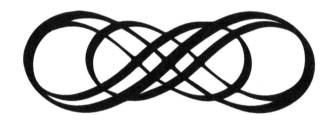

11

THE LIFE-CHANGING POWER OF WRITING A BOOK

LYNDA GOLDMAN

About the Author:

Lynda Goldman became an author by accident, when a colleague asked her to participate in writing and self-publishing a book.

Forty-four books later, her most recent book, *Write to Heal: 7 Steps to Write and Publish a Wellness Book that Heals More People, Makes You the Authority, and Leaves Your Legacy*, became an instant #1 Amazon bestseller in three countries at the same time.

Lynda was published by three major publishers, Prentice Hall, Houghton Mifflin and Oxford University Press, while teaching at the college level for 15 years.

For over 10 years she was a sought-after copywriter in the natural health industry, a speaker at natural products expos, and a ghostwriter for her clients.

She then founded Wellness Ink, where she publishes health and wellness books.

Her popular online course, Author in an Hour, and her book coaching and mastermind groups, help wellness providers, coaches and entrepreneurs write and publish their books, and get #1 Amazon bestsellers, using her secret formula.

Click here to get your **free roadmap to your book**: 7 Steps to Write Your Health and Wellness book

(equally valuable for any non-fiction book)

Website: www.WellnessInk.com

THE LIFE-CHANGING POWER OF WRITING A BOOK

"Books change lives, both for the readers and for the authors."- Lynda Goldman

Books have always had a special place in my life. In fact, reading books and then writing 44 of them have probably been the biggest influence on my health, my business, and my life.

I can still remember the day I fell in love with reading. I was about 6 or 7, lying in bed on a rainy November day, gripped by the suspense in Nancy Drew's *The Secret Staircase.*

At one point I remember thinking, "Wow, I love reading." I was hooked on reading for life.

But my catalyst for *writing* books was quite different. When I was quite young, my father frequently said to me, "Children in Europe have written books and symphonies by the age of 3. What have you ever accomplished?"

Not much, I had to admit. But it got me thinking.

Little did I know that I would later write not just one book, but more than 40, and still counting.

In fact, my earliest desire was to become an artist. I loved drawing, painting, crafts, sculpture, and anything to do with creativity and working with my hands.

However, my parents had other plans for me. They pushed me hard to become a lawyer, to follow in my father's footsteps

(apparently, writing books and symphonies was to be done before the age of 5, before you had a REAL profession.)

Instead, I defied my parents and went into fine arts. I enjoyed every moment of university but had no idea how to make a living afterwards – just as my mother predicted.

The first publisher

With a fine arts degree and not many job prospects, I got a teaching degree and a job teaching English as a Second Language at the college level. One day a colleague approached all the staff members about co-authoring a textbook.

They all said, "You'll never get a publisher."

I was the junior staff member, and completely naïve. I answered, "I've never written a book, but I'll give it a try."

We wrote our first book together and self-published 2000 copies. Those were the days long before Amazon and digital publishing. We had to pay several thousand dollars to have the cover and pages designed and print a large number of copies to be cost effective.

Our first book caught the eye of an acquisitions editor at Prentice Hall, one of the world's largest textbook publishers. They were looking for teachers to write language textbooks, saw our self-published book, and offered us a publishing contract for a 6-level series of books.

Our dilemma was that the offer came in just as a truck rolled in to deliver 2000 more copies of our book, after we had successfully sold most of the first print run.

It was crazy for us to have hesitated even for a moment. *Canadian Concepts* became a landmark series because before that, all the ESL books were from the US or the UK, and Canadian teachers wanted to teach about Canada. The books are still selling twenty years after the last edition was published. The early success led to the publisher asking for several other series for different markets. We were then offered a contract with Houghton Mifflin US to write an American series.

A few years later I was offered a contract with Oxford University Press, the world's most prestigious educational publisher, to write a business book, "You're Hired. Now What?"

I then wrote and self-published, "How to Make a Million Dollar First Impression" which had over 7 printings, and I sold the foreign rights to 10 countries. Along with "Prescription for Success", a book for the health industry, I launched a speaking and training business, where I taught business etiquette skills to sales people at many of the top pharmaceutical and insurance companies. I also sold thousands of copies of the books to these companies.

The "health nut" copywriter and ghost writer

I decided to stop teaching and began writing full time for clients. As a long-time "health nut" I specialized in natural health, and launched my copywriting business.

Many of my clients wanted to write a book, but didn't have the time or ability, so I ghostwrote books under their names.

The truth is that almost every health and wellness professional, coach and entrepreneur wants to become an author to gain authority and help more people, but many don't have the time or expertise to write their book.

Hiring a ghostwriter is an obvious option, but it's not cheap. Fees for a high-quality ghostwriter begin at $30,000 and can soar to $100,000!

That's when I decided to bridge the gap by creating an online course that guides people, step-by-step, to writing their own book. However, there were many courses about how to write a book. I decided to specialize by offering a course on how to write a health and wellness book. I did a pilot course and had great success with a small group, while honing my teaching process.

Then I launched my first full course and made $22,000 in one week. I knew there was a market for teaching how to write a wellness book, but the launch was very stressful and exhausting. I was wondering what to do next, when I found my business coach, Susan.

She taught me how to set up mastermind groups where I can guide students to write and publish their books. I give them a full online course, and then we meet to discuss their individual books. I discovered that having a coach makes all the difference in seeing a project to fruition, and that's what I provide for my clients.

My coaching and guidance give my students the immense satisfaction of writing and publishing their own books, at a fraction of the price of hiring a ghostwriter.

They learn a simple process for writing their book, and many go on to write more than one book. I've also coached them to create Amazon bestsellers, and everyone who has used my system has had a #1 bestseller or #1 new release.

Books change lives – for the author, and the reader

Most people approach me because they have a burning passion to share their wisdom, but have no idea how to get started, or worry they are not good enough writers.

Writing a book can be a scary process when you've never done it before. And publishing today is both easier and more fraught with peril than ever before. There are endless numbers of "publishing companies" on the Internet, ready to grab several months worth of your mortgage (or enough to buy a small house), to publish your book. It gives me great satisfaction to guide my clients to publishing their books successfully on their own, at a fraction of the price, yet at a very high quality.

That's my idea of success: focusing your skills and talents to help more people get what they want, while building a business that brings you joy every day.

My mission is to guide more people write the book that's locked inside them. I love working with my forthcoming authors, helping them shape their books and bring them to life.

I also set up a publishing company, Wellness Ink, and publish some of my clients' book, and even help them get foreign sales.

My advice to anyone who wants to write and publish a book: Get guidance. It can make a world of difference when you get stuck and have questions. Every successful business person needs a coach, and you need one as well to write your book.

I look forward to accompanying you on the journey to your book!

I guarantee that writing and publishing your book will change your life, as well as the lives of people who read it.

You can start your journey with the free road map, at www. Wellnessink.com

12

GETTING TO THE BOTTOM

TREVOR PERRY

About the Author:

Trevor was born in a small town in the outback of Australia. He was raised on a vineyard from the age of four. His youth was spent pondering the mysteries of the universe, and generally finding mischief in all its forms - without the convenience of television.

Knowing his math skills were some of his best talents, Trevor was guided into accounting. While at college, he discovered computers (which immediately became his passion) and the day eventually came where he was employed as a computer consultant. He began travelling regularly across the United States as a speaker on many technical midrange subjects for user group meetings, seminars and conferences.

Now residing on Long Island in New York, Trevor is becoming acquainted with all the wonders of Manhattan and the north east. Having been through an interesting journey of discovery himself, Trevor compiled many of the life lessons he had learned into several motivational sessions and returned to speaking with a newfound energy and passion.

Trevor's Australian heritage and unique sense of humor provide for a different perspective. His sessions are fast-paced, challenging and require only that you sit back and enjoy the ride as your new perspective is cultivated.

Website: www.TrevorPerrySpeaker.com

GETTING TO THE BOTTOM

All my life, I have tried to be brave, bold, adventurous, and open to trying new things. In recent years, I have stopped complaining about horrible "cheese" and been brave to taste all the cheeses I have been offered. Surprisingly, I am enjoying my cheese "adventure".

To determine if I engage in an adventure or make a decision, I have always applied a risk-check. Obviously, I will only be in this situation if I consider the possible results to be positive or beneficial. I then consider all the bad things and determine the worst thing that could happen in that adventure or with that decision. If the worst that could happen is acceptable, then it is easy to make that decision. It's a simple approach, but it requires me to research well, and addresses potential fear.

There are so many things in life that are scary. When I was in my mid-20s, I parachuted three times, and discovered it is one of the most amazing experiences you can ever have in your life. Flying under a parachute is incredibly serene and the first few times your entire body and mind are coming to grips with your senses responding to something overwhelming. I was scared, I was afraid, but I applied my risk-check and I was able to parachute. It was absolutely worth pushing through the fear to get to that positive outcome.

Later in my life, when I was diagnosed with diabetes, my brain was checked with an MRI. The position in which I was lying required foam to be placed around my ears, and my head forced into a stable position inside the MRI machine.

It was a suffocating experience, and following, I became claustrophobic in many situations. This caused me to be fearful of more than I had been in the past.

Many years ago, I created an "I wanna" list - consider it a bucket list. At the top was "I want to bungee". I had researched, and I knew all the facts. There is no huge jerk at the bottom of the bungee - remember, you are connected to, what is essentially, a rubber band. If you remain attached and stretch that band, to its limits, it slows you down before it returns to its initial form. Bungee is considered very safe and the incidences of death from bungee has reduced to a very small number. My risk-check had been done for years, yet I had not purposely taken the chance to bungee. And after the onset of claustrophobia, I felt very reticent to engage.

Then, I found myself in Auckland. Under the Auckland Bridge is one of the most popular bungee jumps. It was time. I decided to use my risk-check to address my qualms and bought a ticket. The day dawned with gorgeous sunny weather. I could not turn back.

The one thing I had not counted on was my fear of heights. The height of the bungee under the Auckland bridge is 43 meters - just around a 140-foot drop. I walked with the group 800 meters (half a mile) underneath the bridge to the jump platform. I was fitted with the harness around my legs and around my chest (used when we are pulled back up). When it was time. I walked to the edge of the plank, looked down, and immediately my knees started knocking! Yes, that physically happened... I turned ghost-white as all the blood drained out of me. The "pusher" offered to nudge me over the edge, but I balked. I went back to the seating area and watched the success of the other jumpers.

When everyone else had completed their jumps, the staff asked if I would like to go, but I was blocked. I could not push through the fear that was consuming me. I spent the majority of the walk back to the hotel beating myself up. This had been on my "I wanna" list for so long, and when it counted, I balked. Of course, I considered this a colossal failure. The discussion in my head was how I could just take it off my "I wanna" list. Yet, I had committed to this as the number one item on my list for almost a decade. I was torn.

I am not sure when it was, but somewhere on that walk home, I resorted to my risk-check. I had seen other people bungee, they were alive and high on the experience. I became determined to bungee. Back at the hotel, I called and was able to book the same experience for the next day. I was determined, but still had to address what had happened.

It became obvious that my brain was very clear on the positive results. It was my fear of heights that broke my resolve. I was determined to address it, maybe something as simple as not looking down? My commitment was strong, and I focused on the end results. I reminded myself of the amazement I felt flying while parachuting and even considered the bragging rights I would get from a successful bungee. If any fear surfaced, I focused on positivity, reminding myself how great the feeling would be upon success.

Well… I did it! I was determined not to let the height defeat me again. I talked to the "pusher" and told him I would close my eyes and shuffle out to the edge of the plank. I asked him if he could tell me when I was at the end, and he did. I raised my arms and took a swan dive off the platform. It was an amazing three seconds of free fall!

I made a commitment, purposely worked to honor that commitment, pushed through my fear, and the experience was one of the most incredible moments in my life.

The lessons I learned from this experience have been applied to many decisions and actions in my life since then - from very small to massive, from inconsequential to important. From continuing experience, these simple lessons are successful.

1. Commit
   - write your goal and share it
2. Risk-check
   - evaluate and accept the worst that can happen
3. Wallow in success
   - consider the positive end result
4. Push through fear
   - remove the limits you place on yourself
**5. Do! **
   - Engage fully in your decision

Whether a small decision, an amazing adventure, or you are contemplating a life changing event, be bold, be brave, and engage in an extraordinary life.

You ARE extraordinary

13

LEADER OF THE PACK:

How a single dad of five led his kids, his business and himself from disaster to success.

MATT SWEETWOOD

About the Author:

We live in extremely challenging times. Technology, artificial intelligence, and globalization have had a profound effect on business and our working environment today. Societal changes and financial pressures have made our relationships, marriages and personal life harder to find comfort and happiness in.

Matt Sweetwood has over 30 years of entrepreneurial experience and is a thought leadership and personal branding expert. He was the U.S. CEO of a Social Media Network that helps people build personal brands. As president of Unique Photo, he was credited with the reinvention of the modern camera store, as well as the country's largest in-store photography education program. However, by far, his greatest achievement is having raised five successful children to adulthood as a single dad.

Matt was the winner of the 2014 CMO Club President's Award, the 2015 Aish Center's Continuity award and the Photography Industry's 2016 person of the year. Recently he published a book titled: "Leader of the Pack: How a single dad of five led his kids, his business and himself from disaster to success.

He is a life coach and is a regular contributor on national TV in the social media, photography, business and parenting arenas and he is a regular contributor to Entrepreneur magazine. Most of all as a professional speaker he is authentic, charismatic with a true heart for his audience.

Website: www.MSweetwood.com

LEADER OF THE PACK:

How a single dad of five led his kids, his business and himself from disaster to success.

Leader of the Pack is the story of a man who, like many men, had been going through his life apparently content and positively clueless, and who found himself tethered to a tornado as his marriage descended into violence and madness. Surviving courts and cops and chaos, and a crazy-challenging business, he unexpectedly ended up being the only parent of five small children—ranging in ages from only 18 months to 8 years old—at a time when most men didn't even know how to change a diaper.

It is my story.

In it, I detail the transformation I underwent from sole breadwinner and "backup" parent to sole parent, from a beaten abused shell of a man to the strong, confident, and spiritual person I am today, a nationally recognized spokesman for single parents and entrepreneurs.

Though the facts of my story may be different than those of others, my feelings are the same for single fathers everywhere. We are frustrated. We're no longer just the backup parent, the ringer sent in when Mom isn't available—though that was all we had ever been trained for when it came to parenting. It's not that we don't love our children. We do, but that and $5 will get you a latte at Starbucks.

We are told by the many voices of (and silent looks from)

counselors, teachers, social workers, judges, and our mothers, sisters, and ex-wives that we aren't as capable of raising kids as a woman. We may even feel that assessment is true. We feel helpless and undermined and, above all, alone in this.

But we are not alone.

A quarter of all American single-parent households are headed by men. We need to own that position, be proud of it, figure out the best way to make it work and, above all, add our voices to a swelling chorus of support for our brothers who find themselves in our shoes.

We must learn to parent like a dad, and that does not mean being only half of a team. In my life, and in the lives of millions of men today, we are *the* parent. Where there were two, now there is one, and we must be enough.

Lives depend on it…our kids' lives.

We can win our kid's affection and respect, raise them to be happy and healthy people, and manage to have a big, fun, and exciting life while we were doing so. Life isn't over for us. In fact, it is just beginning, and beyond the doors swinging open lies a road we never could have foreseen—one filled with adventure and laughter and even sex.

I surely never would have believed it. On the day my life changed forever, I looked wildly around for any means of escape, but all I saw were their pale and frightened faces, staring up at me. Five little kids. The oldest was only 8, and the youngest still a toddler. My kids—all mine now. Their mother had staged one last violent, terrifying episode and left us forever. Where there were once two parents, there was now only one.

It felt like something had torn a large hole in my chest and ripped out my lungs. I couldn't breathe. Then the breath rushed back in and I heard the most heartbreaking crying. It wasn't until later that I realized the sound was coming from me.

***

Wheaties boxes featured Major League baseball players on them. Barbie dolls had impossibly tiny waists and pointy breasts. Dad might don his checkered apron and silly chef's hat to flip a burger, but holiday dinners were always cooked by Mom. Women had the babies. Men paced the waiting room. The kids' boo-boos got kissed by Mommy, and Daddy got the report of their misdeeds when he came home from work.

That was the world in which I grew up, and though gender lines have blurred (Bruce Jenner is now a woman, for God's sake) and there are enough "Mr. Moms" around for the phrase to be heard less often, not everything has changed, even now.

In the 1980s when my wife and I were having kids, inroads were being made regarding parenting roles. More women were working, and daycare became a normal part of life. But as the man, I was still expected to bring home most of the bacon and as a woman, my wife was expected largely to raise the kids.

We had plenty of those.

My wife stayed home with them, and I went forth to earn the paycheck needed to feed all those hungry mouths. Things unfolded as expected, everybody was relatively happy and healthy...or so it appeared.

Our lives were about to be upended as totally as though an Indonesian tsunami had crashed over us.

My wife, Charlotte, never the nicest woman on the planet, finally dropped the mask she had been hiding behind and revealed her true self to me and to our kids. She was a monster—violent, abusive and downright terrifying. Everything I thought I knew was suddenly a lie, and I found myself struggling to breathe under the weight of her fury, while trying to save my kids without a life vest myself.

I had been her first target in the family. Charlotte belittled me constantly: I was fat and worthless, and I disgusted her. She mocked my manhood and came at me with cutting insults or wheedling endearments, and it was hard to tell which was the most damaging. She hated me, she loved me, she was leaving, I should get out, she couldn't live anymore, I shouldn't be allowed to go on living.

My wife had been increasingly unreasonable, shrieking at the kids over the smallest slights, bellowing like a bully until they were white-faced in a corner, telling them they were useless and stupid, and she had never loved them. She hit and kicked walls and the kids, threatening to kill herself. She raged, pivoting between uncontrollable screaming, harsh laughter, and hoarse sobbing. She smashed our lives as surely as she smashed the crockery.

She left in increments—disappearing and reappearing, each time with threats of violence, tormenting the kids, leaving a trail of tears and broken furniture in her wake.

I found myself the single parent of all those children, grabbing for any branch so my children wouldn't disappear in a mudslide of fear and confusion, trying to get up out of the muck myself to be strong for them, trying to work and sleep and provide food and a crying shoulder for my traumatized children and, above all, trying to create order out of chaos.

It was the most important work I would ever do and, hands down, the hardest.

But I strapped one baby to my front, another to my back, grabbed hands, elbows, and shirt collars of the other three kids and started down a road I never thought I'd find myself walking.

Along the way, I found myself in the offices of counselors and clerics, in hot water and nearly in handcuffs, in police stations and political meetings, and in front of many, many judges.

I had no plans to become either a revolutionary or a pioneer— yet I became both. As one of the few who fought the system for years and won, I gave hope to other men fighting for their kids. I had done it. They could do it.

I was asked about my story so often (people gasped at the tale and then passed it around like a box of Cracker Jacks,) I decided to write a little something online about it. I now have many articles that have gotten thousands of views. I had hit a nerve, one as raw and pulsating as mine were when I began this journey. I want to keep sharing my story because it can help people, and I now understand that is why I went through it in the first place.

Leader of the Pack is the story of how our lives fell apart and how I was able to sweep up the pieces and assemble us back into that most unbreakable unit—a strong family. It is the tale of how this single father of five may have lost his hair along the way but not his sanity...or even his sense of humor...and how a newfound spirituality was the greatest treasure unearthed in his journey.

14

Look up, Grow up, Show up

VERNON BROWN

About the Author:

Vernon Brown was born in Richmond, VA where he resides till this day with his 3-year-old son Logan and his beautiful wife Shawnta for 19 Years. Vernon struggled the first 20 years of his life trying to make sense of where he belonged. Vernon came from an abusive and drug ridden household. He studied Psychology at VCU (Virginia Commonwealth University) and has a certificate in Fine Arts from John Tyler College.

Vernon worked as a model, an actor in NY and as a Personal Trainer for many years. But that was not fulfilling for the change he wanted to see in people. For the past Five years he has studied and coached hundreds of men and women on finding and sustaining their happiness.

"I believe your life truly begins when you make happiness a tangible commodity that is non-negotiable." – Vernon Brown

Through turmoil and tribulations in his own childhood and into adulthood, Vernon Brown had to make a decision that will alter his life and make him who he is today. His gift of empathy and his charismatic personality combined with his knowledge of finding happiness is equal to none.

Your audience will experience an amazing rollercoaster of emotions that not only will leave them at the edge of their seat and hanging to his every word, they will be changed and be able to apply what they learned instantly.

Website: www.WhatsYourHappi.com

Look up, Grow up, Show up

Growing up I was the awkward kid, you know the kid who was "frumpy" looking in appearance and in approach. I spent so much time not fitting in I started to read medical journals when I was in elementary school. Which was a hit with your peers in grade school. This narrative played on through middle school where it changed from being ostracized to being included in daily discussions about how my clothes were not name brand. Or how I I spoke to properly even though they knew I came from a poor family. From those conversations it started getting physical which made the end of my school day a sprint to avoid getting beat up.

When I got to high school being under developed does not go over well with the ladies. I was overweight spent more time reading, drawing and running from bullies like it was a full-time job. Needless to say, I felt absolutely worthless, ignored (unless it was for me to feel some sort of pain) confused as to why I was the butt of every aspect of life. I remember wanting to just stop the pain, it was all I knew in life and I wanted it to end.

Those thoughts got very loud, like a megaphone in your ear loud. All day, every day, in my sleep I would just have dreams where everything was black. I graduated high school and the dreams I had almost became a reality. I had enough and wanted a reprieve. Life changed dramatically for me that summer because I had decided it needed to end. I was tired of carrying that weight.

93

I decided I would make sure things would stop right after I tried my hand at college. I felt free for once, people's words did not have quite the same sting that they had before. Being alone meant more time for me to learn about things I wanted to learn about. All this happened once I committed to ending it all. It was time to enroll and I was excited about life not *being* there anymore

Life has a sense of humor, I know this because that summer I grew 6 inches and gained 80lbs of good weight. I enrolled, and against my advisors warning I double majored in kinetic imagery and psychology (I wanted to learn about motivations for action, why people do what they do). The time spent not fitting in and reading early in life and drawing was my bigger gift than I could have imagined. I was no longer that kid who was the *whitest black* guy who knew too much. I was very well received by classmates because I knew a lot of the answers and asked the great questions that made professors think. I got a thrill that I could retain so much information from the books and lecture and others had to scramble through notes. I had all the information stored in my head, a question would get asked and boom my hand shoots up. It was not always the only hand going up, but I was not shy or afraid to throw it up. No more hesitation, it was like I was a new person.

I was being asked to be in study groups and they wanted me to participate in the discussions in them. I was actually hanging out with people after class, going to dinner with lots of classmates and hanging out over my new friends' houses. This was another world for me all together. The teachers actually called me out for maintaining a high GPA even though I had a demanding schedule. What a spin on things, almost 20 years of the polar opposite. It felt wrong for me to be feeling this.

As I was doing great in school there were so many new things going on that I had never thought possible for me. I was presented with the opportunity to be a model and actor in New York. This was being offered to the guy who was told he would never amount to anything by his own family. The guy who would end up a felony since I had no direction, again by my family and some peers. It was amazing to be in magazines, on videos, on magazine covers and on national TV. This was not something I ever thought imaginable for myself, literally surreal.

It was not 6 years later did I realize I had not made good on my decision. I had not had the time to even consider it again or to even remember what I was feeling then. That initially caused me to feel like a failure. I had committed to a decision and I did not follow through. I completely forgot about how bad life was and was actually enjoying it. That was such a huge failure for me. Then I realized I had not failed. I made a decision and that decision was to end it. That's exactly what I did do. I ended allowing myself to feel hurt because I was not amongst my peers of similar thoughts and ideas. I ended letting other people expectations be the compass on how I lived my life.

I share to say of all the lessons I have learned in life is that sometimes it is your environment that does not support you. Often times it is not you but the people you surround yourself with. Constantly audit every interaction you have with anyone. "How am I feeling when I am with them?", "Are they positive and allow me to be myself" "What am I learning from this person?". These are great questions to get you really examining your people eco-system. The beauty of it is you can change so much about how you show up and perceive the world all by exposing yourself to new people. You do not have to tell the current people in your life you can no longer talk to them, just distance yourself to some degree. The most precious gift we are ever given in this life is time. Ensure you are spending it with people who light you up, open up and challenge you to think differently. It took me 20 years to realize this however it does not need to take you that long. It is your life and lead it the way you want because in snap of the fingers life will pass you by.

15

WHAT IS YOUR THOUGHT PATTERN?

RUBY FRAZIER

About the Author:

Ruby Frazier is a Certified Teacher, Speaker and Coach. For over 10 years Ruby Frazier has studied and implemented transformational success principles and as a sought-after speaker, trainer, and certified coach, Ruby Frazier's, workshops and coaching programs help people breakthrough limitations and achieve greater results than they have known before.

Ruby Frazier offers inspiring workshops to audiences as well as transformational in-depth coaching programs that help clients achieve new heights of success, meaning, and aliveness. She has self-published several books.

Website: www.DramaForSuccess.com

WHAT IS YOUR THOUGHT PATTERN?

As a native of North Carolina, I grew up in the south hearing clichés and sayings that ruled our thinking, such as can't cry over spilled milk, don't judge a book by its cover and my personal favorite sticks and stones may break my bones; but, words will never hurt me. My brain swells in agony as I think of how much words hurt ones mental and emotional wellbeing years and decades past the offense. My skin cringes as I think of the power and impact negative words has when spoken in a disempowering context.

I have a theory, like many other theorists, I believe our thoughts create our realities. No matter what our lives look like or feel like it was created by a thought, which was followed up by an emotion that we assigned an emotion to it. In other words, it was our negative or positive thinking that determines our reality. For example, I may write a paper and get a poor grade on it, and instead of seeing it as poor performance, I start judging and criticizing myself, saying things like I am not good enough, I am not smart enough to do this. The thought I am not good enough lead me to attack my self-worth with the emotion that I am worthless and can't do anything right. Clearly, my thought pattern is giving me the reality that I am experiencing.

Our thoughts attack all areas of our lives, health, finances, love, relationships and other areas of life. Our self-talk whether positive or negative determines the quality of our lives. Positive self -talk lead to a positive self-esteem. On the other hand, negative self-talk could lead to poor self-esteem, illness, loss of interest and a diminished listening of yourself. In the times of trouble, it is important to be kind to yourself and suspend the negative self-judgments and self- criticisms. Remind yourself that you are an amazing human being who is talented and capable of handling any of the challenges life throws at you.

Be aware of the constant negative thoughts that feed on other negative emotions. Refuse to feed and fuel emotions that could lead to anxiety and dis-ease. Pay close attention to what you are thinking and how you feel. Keeping a close eye on what you are thinking could be the key and cure to healthy emotional well-being.

Words are powerful and should be treated with respect for the power they carry. There is nothing in the universe that did not begin as a thought. The thought began in someone's mind and then was manifested as the idea that was imagined. In fact, it would be hard to think about a thing that has not already been imagined. We simply would not have words for it.

Our thoughts, words, and desires often define who we are. As we mature we are told to be mindful of what we say and to whom we share our thoughts and feelings. So where does all of the unexpressed feelings and thoughts go? You have a thought and then you add on an emotion and then a feeling to the thoughts and emotions and that creates a spiraling effect. Most likely, the unexpressed thoughts and feelings turn into fears and anxiety.

Fear (as defined by the famous acronym "false evidence

appearing real") is crippling. Fear block people from doing the things that they are called to do. Facing your fears, give you control. Focus on what is important to you. Fear block purpose and creativity. As business owners and leaders, one must take the time to discover your purpose. Focus on who you are destined to become and challenge yourself to make a difference in the world. As leaders' you cannot allow fear to stop you from being present and following your dream.

All leaders are responsible for knowing the power of words and the magnitude of every thought. When children get into a verbal fight you may hear them chatter sticks and stones may break my bones, but words will never hurt me. They take pride in calling each other names and verbally bashing one another.

Living on purpose has power, presence, and potential for being in action. It requires one to take capture of every thought he or she has. Thoughts will come, both positive and negative. Every leader must take captive of his or her own thought. Granted one cannot keep from having a thought or thoughts, however you can control the meaning and emotions that you will entertain your thoughts with. With constant practice, one can choose not to dwell on negative thought patterns that cause unhappy or unwanted negative feelings.

16

WHEN LOVE IS NOT ENOUGH

CARLOS CINTRON

About the Author:

Recognized for his exceptional communication and presentation skills, Carlos Cintron is among the world's foremost brand builders. Carlos rose to prominence at the beginning of the millennium as part of the TIGI International Creative Team, where he traveled the globe doing shows and seminars inspiring tens of thousands for TIGI/Bed Head Hair Care.

Today, he is Vice President of Orly Amor Enterprises, COO of HWNCC and COO of the Social WOW Factor, where he shares his knowledge and passion on Health and Wellness

Website: www.CarlosCintron.com

WHEN LOVE IS NOT ENOUGH

January 3, 2018

7:28 am

Good morning Carlos, I'm sure by now you know that I have left. I love you and will always love you but I'm sorry, I just can't stay. I really want to talk with you about things. Let's talk when things cool down a little.

7:30 am

I want you to know that I miss you already, but I know in my heart that this is the right thing to do

8:00 am

Elizabeth,
Please call me I just woke up and I'm confused. Please. I can't go to work I'm so broken.

8:07

I'll call you when I can. Can't talk at the moment. I'm sorry

These were the text messages that I woke up to the day my live-in girlfriend of 3 years decided to end our relationship.

Never in my wildest dreams did I expect this behavior from someone I trusted, loved, planned on marrying and start a family with

Devastated, heartbroken, angry, humiliated, betrayed, confused, sad, depressed, how will I get over this!?! This was my daily talk to myself for 2 months, until one day, I came across this quote " Life doesn't happen to you, it happens for you"Tony Robbins.

The moment I started to embrace those words is when the healing began.

I decided to hire a Life Coach to help me make sense of what was happening in my life and it turned out to be a blessing.

SESSION 1. (Acceptance)

LC.
Carlos, I want you to play detective, go back to the beginning of your relationship and look for signs that led to where you are today and write them down.

Carlos.

What is that going to prove?!?

LC.

You'll be amazed at what you will discover, trust me, it's an exercise that will give you clarity.

Carlos.

Ok I'll do it, just promise you will help me get over this pain that I'm feeling.

LC.

There is no instant cure for what you are going through but

if you do the work you will discover that everything is exactly the way it supposed to be.

That evening I put pen to paper, I wrote, and wrote for what seemed like hours, my journal was 10 pages full of detective work. When I was done I read through my notes. Holy Shit! Love is blind, was my final conclusion. I couldn't believe that I had turned a blind eye to avoid confrontation and keep the peace.

SESSION 2 (The Breakthrough)

LC.

So, Carlos what were you able to discover?

Carlos

First, I learned that love is blind! There were signs from day one that I chose to ignore and if I would have paid attention things would be different today.

LC

How so

Carlos.

There's a lesson we must learn from any relationship that falls apart. The lesson that I learned is, I can't control anyone and I'm not responsible for someone else's behavior.

LC.

There are two valuable lessons you must learn in life.1. Relationships are a privilege not a right.

2. You're either a participant or an observer, be the observer you'll gain more wisdom. If you can master these two you will have long lasting relationships with family, friends, and partner.

Carlos.

So how do I overcome this pain that I'm feeling.

LC.

Time my friend, you need to focus on the present. Here's a quote for you " Stop cheating on your future with the past, it's over and has been for some time!" You need to calm your mind try meditating and exercising.

Those words resonated, I found myself meditating and listening to relationship videos. I was determined to shut the doors of the past and to be open to new beginnings

I started to set goals for betterment, I wrote mantra's and daily affirmations that I posted all over my apartment. Here are some of my favorites.

"As I let go of the need to arrange my life god and the universe bring abundant good to me"

"Accept things as they are not as they should be"

"I am in control of my life and today I choose to live like there's no tomorrow"

" It's not who we are that holds us back its who we think we're not"

"Today I will judge nothing that occurs"

It's been 10 months since I discovered my true self and perspective on life and my relationships have taken a whole new meaning, it's called PURPOSE!

17

A LAWYER... JUST LIKE YOU -
A girl's journey in the footsteps of her mentor

REGINA FAUL PLL

About the Author:

Regina is a successful lawyer practicing employment and labor law in NYC. She started her career as a union side labor lawyer and moved to representing companies over 10 years ago. She is an avid golfer, loves to ride motorcycles, and loves to learn new things.

Regina is a Reiki practitioner and believes in the energy that connects us to each other. She lives with her family in Westchester County, NY.

Website: www.ReginaFaul.com

A LAWYER... JUST LIKE YOU -
A girl's journey in the footsteps of her mentor

"Don't go in there…. Mr. C. is working and doesn't like to be disturbed…" My four-year-old eyes contemplated her, I shrugged and walked down the stairs, looked over my shoulder and ran around the corner right in to the room he was in. There he was, sitting on the couch, papers and books everywhere, using a tv tray table to work. I climbed on to a chair, swinging my fat little legs I asked whatcha doin'? He did not glance up. Or answer me. I asked again, whatcha doin'? This time he looked up, glowering at me…reluctantly he barked, "working". Not to be deterred I asked some other question…he looked up again and I saw this smirk…I knew I was IN! He allowed me to stay so long as I was quiet. I was…for a four-year-old. Of course, I asked more questions and of course he answered me. Finally, my sister came in and made me leave to go home, but not before I planted a big kiss on his cheek. I loved this cranky old (50!) man. And he loved me. A year or so later, this time at my own home, he and his wife were visiting my parent (we lived a few short blocks away). He was sitting in our den (TV room) with my dad. I squirmed my way onto his lap. He crustily said to me, "Little girl, what are you going to be, what are you going to do with your life?" I looked at him quizzically and said, what do you do? He told me he was a lawyer. Without missing a beat, I declare, Well, that's what I'll be. And so, it began.

Of course, throughout my young life, I pretended I would grow up to be a teacher, or a nurse (like my mom) or an executive (like my dad) or a farmer (like the one's I'd see when we visited museums like Phillipsburg Manor or Old

Sturbridge Village), but I never truly waivered from that declaration to Mr. C. It was always in my heart. I graduated high school and went to colleges as pre-law. Mistake. I took business courses and computer courses, all of which interested me. None of the pre-law stuff did. At all. Mr. C had told me to call him when I was ready, and he'd help me go to law school. He was an influential man in the legal field. (who knew!) I called him in my senior year of college – even though I saw him at least monthly and he always asked – what are you going to be? And I answered - A lawyer, just like you!

I started law school in the night program because my grades were not good enough (3.7 college average) to get into the day program. I was disappointed, but I persevered. During my first year I was hospitalized for asthma at least three times. The last time was during finals week. I missed my finals but got to take them a week or two after the rest of my class. I passed first year – barely. During that summer I accelerated, taking classes over the summer break while others were interning at law firms. I started my second year as a day student. I worked all through college and first year. When I moved to the day program I had to quit my job. I had so much time on my hands, it felt strange. So, I clerked for a professor and then for the Dean of the law school. Mr. C. and I would travel home together on the evenings when he taught late. He would advise me, tell me the classes to take, the professors to take - and the ones to avoid. He had to convince me to take his class in labor law (he was the greatest labor lawyer ever). I did it, not happily because I was going to concentrate my career on mergers and acquisitions and didn't really have time for labor law (eye roll here). But he persisted, not letting up until I agreed. First class, five minutes in…without looking up from his podium, he calls my name, in his gravelly voice, and barked a question at me…I don't recall my answer because I thought I was going to DIE! Somehow, I gave the right answer. I never got called on again. But something changed. I knew. From that moment. I was hooked. I knew I had found what would be the best area of law, what would keep me interested for 30 plus years, I found my passion. Sadly, he became ill at the end semester and never finished the class. He passed away. I was devastated. I honored him by taking every labor law related class I could. When I graduated, I worked as a union side attorney, practicing traditional labor law, handling 100's of labor arbitrations, negotiating hundreds of agreements and crafting myself as a tough but fair adversary. I was in the trenches, with mostly men. I was tough, scary at times, a force to be reckoned with, as I'm told. I am a fighter, it did not matter that I was a girl among men, I was there to win. I was never looked down upon, I was not often treated differently because I was a female. If I was, God help that person… I always had integrity. I had a reputation, one I am proud of and have to this day. I am smart, honest, and fair.

I stayed with union side law for nearly 20 years and then made the major change to management side. I started with not one single client of my own. Within the first few days, I received a call from one of the companies I often fought against. Mr. D. and Mr. R. wanted me to be their lawyer. I was surprised and excited. The phone kept ringing. Many of my adversaries wanted me to be their lawyer too. Fast forward 5 years, I had a large client base and was named a partner in my firm. I have moved firms a few times but have finally found a home where I will stay. I am now the Chair of my practice group, Labor and Employment law. I could not be happier. Still, to this day, practicing labor law and employment law makes me happy, fuels my soul and provides me a great life. My priorities in life have changed over the last several years. I have found it better to be more thoughtful and connected to my soul than to be a fighter. But the fighter never goes completely away, it is a part of who I am – and I wear it proudly. Love, kindness, gratitude, forgiveness, respect, honesty, are all the things I strive for and bring to my life and to my law practice. That's what makes me different. And being all those things make me more effective and more well received.

Along with my parents, Mr. C. has stayed with me, guiding me through my career. Remarkably, I followed in his footsteps. I still strive to be as great and as loved as he was.

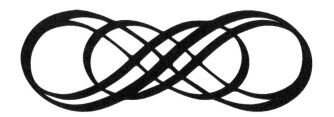

18

THE RIPPLE EFFECT

KAREN MAYO

About the Author:

Karen Mayo, an award winning international best-selling author of "Mindful Eating". Karen has guided numerous people to losing inches, pounds and medications through better eating habits. As a natural whole foods' chef Karen fulfills her passion of partnering with people who are committed to improving their health and lifestyle of their families. Karen is board certified Integrative Nutrition health and lifestyle coach, member of American Association of Drugless Practitioners, certified in fitness and sports nutrition specialist by The National Strength and Fitness Association. Double certified in Corporate Wellness by Vital Advantage and Kelly Wellness. Certified in Hormone Health and Auto-Immune Disorders by the AADP. Karen is certified in Brain Health by Dr. Daniel Amen. Karen has a private health coaching practice specializing in an effective diet, and lifestyle changes to help her clients lose weight, have more energy, sleep better, and become more confident in all aspects of life in addition to leading corporate health and wellness workshops offering group programs and private individual health and nutrition coaching to Fortune 500 companies and their families.

Website: www.KarenMayo.net

THE RIPPLE EFFECT

My sister, a single mom made a tough but brave decision to enroll into the United States Army. My nephew couldn't go with her to boot camp; she asked if Scott could stay with me. I said "Of course." Prior to Scott coming to stay with me, he was eating everything from fast food to foods loaded with preservatives, MSG, and genetically modified corn-based foods such as his favorite snack in a bag with food coloring red 40 and yellow 5 & 6. He was also diagnosed with ADHD and taking medication. His grades were a "C" at best and he was sliding by every year. Scott was eating unhealthy foods loaded with chemicals. No wonder he wasn't thinking at his best, which his grades clearly demonstrated.

We established a new routine, I made his breakfast with things such as eggs and smoothies, packed his lunch almost every day with a sandwich made with 12 grain bread, sliced chicken or turkey with lettuce. And then a healthy dinner with a big salad every night, topped with chicken or steak and sometimes pizza. Yes, you read that right. If you are eating a big healthy leafy green salad you can eat a slice of pizza. Snacks consisted of popcorn, nuts and chocolate in moderation.

Everything was going well and then one day I get a phone call from one of Scotts teachers and said she and the other teachers would like to set up a meeting with me. I had no idea why. I thought *"maybe Scott really does need his medication."* He did not bring his medication when he came to stay with

115

me.

I went to the school the day of the meeting I walked through the door way and I said to myself "OMG! I'm in really big trouble!" Sitting at the table was the principle, vice-principal, Scott's teachers and when diagnosed with ADHD there is another set of teachers and then a person from the school district. On que the teacher who called me said "don't worry Karen you're not in trouble go ahead and have a seat." I said, "Thank you very much for telling me that" and then something magical happened. I sat at a table and listened to Scott's teachers tell me how pleased they are with him. Scott had earned a place on the honor roll and received a certificate from the Blue Mountain Middle School for straight A's in math. His math teacher told me that she was in awe of him when she would watch him multiply three numbers by three numbers and arrive at the correct answer without using scratch paper. I couldn't say anything. I just stared at his teachers in shock. "What are you doing with him?" they asked. The teachers were finding it hard to understand how Scott could have such a major turnaround when they looked at his past records. A "C" student at best, always sliding by every school year to straight "A's" and honor roll. I said, "This is my first-time taking care of teenager, I was just doing what my mother did with my sisters and me growing up. I'm feeding him healthy, nutritious food. Scott was eating much healthier, so his brain and body were healthy."

My nephew, off medications and getting good grades. Hhmmm. Love love love this!!

Scott also bloomed in other areas. He played baseball on a

Little League team and received his first trophy, and he was also an active Boy Scout.

I thought, If *I can do this with a sixth grader, then I need to get out and talk to people about how easy it is to eat healthy and reduce their medications. That small changes every day can make a big difference.*

My journey led me to Institute for Integrative Nutrition, which is the world's largest nutrition school per graduating class. Powerful teachers who are the leading doctors, PhDs, researchers, and authorities in nutrition and healthcare today.

After losing my mom to cancer and my grandparents to chronic illness diseases, the way we eat maters. I felt a very strong desire in my body to do something about helping others. It is a divine responsible that I wanted to be able to impact on a lot of people in a quick manner. I started writing my Amazon international bestselling book "Mindful Eating" which is my perspective on what I have learned through research and lived through experiences of my own life. I share with you a few things we never learned in health class and a few things we did learn in science class.

I know this way of eating works because my clients are losing weight, thinking more clearly, feeling more energetic, and, best of all, some of them have been able to reduce their medications. Here are two of my clients and their experience of working with me.

We bought Karen Mayo's book, Mindful Eating for our employee's as an employee benefit, and also engaged Karen to do a ten-week eating revisionist program. Since employee's have embraced the fundamentals of Mindful Eating, they all report, more energy, weight loss, clearer thinking, and the best part is that it is NOT a diet per se. Mindful eating is about being more thoughtful about what foods we put in our body, their origins, the possible negative consequences of certain things, and trying to eat as little processed foods as possible.

Karen's in-depth knowledge of simple ideas for handling physical symptoms with better, more mindful eating makes this a program that you can live with for the rest of your life. As a recovering chocolate addict, the principles of this book is helping me and others every day make better food choices.

-Randy Weis, CEO, RD Weis Companies, Elmsford, NY

Before working with Karen, I was 60 lbs. overweight and in a desperate place with my health. I was stuck in a cycle of sugar and caffeine addiction and felt worn out both mentally and physically. I had spent too many years trying to tackle this by myself and I knew I needed help. My husband heard about Karen through his friend who was reading her book "Mindful Eating: Thirty Days to A Whole New You." A few weeks later, I started my journey with Karen.

My goals when starting the Mindful Eating program were to achieve a healthy weight, break patterns and behaviors that were holding me back, embrace a new lifestyle, and rediscover my natural energy. I am results driven and Karen helped me set realistic expectations. More importantly, she helped me push through setbacks with an abundance of patience and kindness.

I would describe Karen as incredibly positive, encouraging, and knowledgeable. I had a weekly call with Karen and that made all the difference. Those weekly calls provided accountability and a space to ask my many questions. Karen took me for who I was, where I was, without judgement and never left my side through this process.

After working with Karen for nearly a year, I now know that this lifestyle change is possible. Today, I'm down 50 lbs., my digestion has improved, I'm thoughtful about what I put in my body, and I have natural energy that I didn't know was possible; free of caffeine and sugar. Working with Karen has changed my life!

-Julie, pregnant wife and loving my life.

There comes a time in one's life as it has in mine, that you want to make a difference for humanity. We all make promises every day to ourselves, to our families, to our colleagues and to our communities. As a young girl growing up on a farm in Pennsylvania with my mom, dad and two sisters, I learned about eating. A hard-working family, living the American dream during the 70's. We had pigs, cows and a big half acre size garden, which had everything from green beans, tomatoes, broccoli, cucumbers to lettuces and peppers. My sister, Dawn and I used to pick weeds on the weekends and feed them to the cows and pigs, not our favorite thing to do as teenage girls but looking back on it now, how I was raised was a wonderful way to grow up. My mother's cooking was the best and I learned a lot from her. I have had a widely varied career path working as a bartender, server, sous chef, model, actress, product spokesperson, licensed real estate agent, home mortgage banker, motivational speaker and executive recruiter. Along the way I always kept my family roots to a healthy way of eating. My passion is sharing my knowledge with others how making minor changes in eating healthy can make a big difference in healing their bodies.

I graduated, board certified by Institute of Integrative Nutrition as an Integrative Nutrition Holistic Health Practitioner, certified by the American Association of Drugless Practitioners and a member of International Association of Health Coaches. Double Certified Corporate Wellness Presenter. Certified Personal Trainer and Sports Nutrition Specialist through the National Council On Strength and Fitness. I study Pilates. I offer programs to clients ranging from a thirty-day kick-start to a healthier you as a short-term goal to getting your own Mindful Eating Certificate as a long-term goal. I also offer my clients one-on-one coaching, as well as group coaching with wellness workshops, lunch and learns, wellness presentations to corporations, cooking classes, grocery store tours, health-food store tours, and so much more. I have most recently become a bee-keeper. All the integrated pieces of a life's work of art coming together in healthy living. If a person is taught to fish, they will eat for life.

19
FAT GIRL CHRONICLES

ALEXA CERVANTES OLIVA

About the Author:

Executive Director of BOWA World and & BOWA Studios, has been developing and delivering programs on leadership, employee development, communication, sales, and organizational structuring for over two decades. She is a brand strategist who graduated from the University of Miami with a B.A. in Business Administration and Marketing. She has produced many training programs that have facilitated growth to numerous global brands in a wide array of industries and has a passion for creating awareness programs for community outreach campaigns. She specializes in facilitating leadership and marketing trainings that focus on developing others, communication skills, and relationship building.

Alexa has been on the Board of Directors for the National

Association of Women Business Owners, Global One, Mindbuzz Enterprises, Regional Policy Council for Miami Dade County, and more. Today she is the founder of Motivational Missions, a 501(c)(3) not-for-profit organization, which empowers, educates, and motivates children through educational/leadership seminars and awareness campaigns around the world. Responsibilities include sponsor relations, marketing campaigns, and overall coordination and logistics for the various tours. Learn more at www.AlexaOliva.com.

Website: www.AlexaCervantesOliva.com

FAT GIRL CHRONICLES

Ever since I was 8 years old I can remember being self-conscious about my weight. I remember comparing myself to my classmates and other family members and noticing I was considerably bigger. At this time, I was only 10-15 pounds heavier than I should be, but for my family, my culture, and my mother especially, it was necessary that you look good. Being Colombian, looking good is a vital aspect of everyday life.

My mother was very adamant about not just looking good but treating your body as a temple and making sure you would eat properly and exercise. Because my mother also had a slight weight issue throughout her life, she made sure never to have unhealthy choices at home, which made them seem oh so much more attractive when I could get my hands on them. I remember going to my friends' houses and always seeing their pantries so filled with all kinds of junk food that I never saw in my house. But even to this point I never really had a love for food nor was I extremely overweight.

It wasn't until 1992 right before Hurricane Andrew hit South Florida when I spent a week at the Dolphin Hotel in Disney World and ate so much that I gained 10 pounds that one week. Right after I got back from that trip I had some massive personal issues that changed my life forever and I immediately ballooned to 275 pounds. I was officially morbidly obese; a struggle that would continue for over two decades.

I didn't fit comfortably in an airplane seat. I struggled with what others thought of me when I ate in public. I worried if I was too big for amusement park rides. Carrying weight around with you is more than the physical burden of the weight. It's also the mental, emotional, and spiritual toll that the weight and the anxiety of the weight causes you.

I started noticing that I was the biggest girl in the room; the fattest woman everywhere I went. This is also when I started to realize that fat girls get punished with fashion. All the clothes for fat women have flowers and prints and pleats and are just horrible. I would always tell myself, "This is the punishment I get for eating the way that I do." And for a lot of years I would try and buy a bathing suit and when I would see them on me in the dressing room I would be totally disgusted, and I would say, "This is what you get for being fat; so you can't have one."

I also started getting scared that I was going to lose my husband because he started with someone who was a size 8 and now he had a full size 22 that was more concerned about her children and didn't care about her looks. I began being ashamed of being the wife of such a good-looking husband and this anxiety just caused me to eat more. This is where I think I started to develop my stress-eating pattern and started fad dieting: Atkins, Phen Phen, Calorie Counting, Weight Watchers, Slimfast, and more.

I did get back to the gym that I had been avoiding for 15 years, but that didn't help or didn't work, and I continued stress eating. And this just started creating a pattern and a cycle of ballooning up and ballooning down and never realizing that I needed to be fit; that fitness (whether you're a size 2 or a size 22) is what makes you feel healthy not just the weight loss.

However, throughout this, I was lucky enough to have a husband who did support me (my fears were only in my own mind). He really didn't care what weight I was. And if he did, he never showed me the least bit concern about my weight or my lack of energy put toward my outward appearance.

During this time also, we started our business and I realized I had to dress corporate to go to a lot of business meetings. This was almost torture living in Florida, as most of the corporate stuff was long sleeves and jackets, and makes you feel sweaty, and yucky, and as a size 22, definitely kills your sexy.

However, because I felt so big and ugly, I did start working a lot harder on my relationship building skills and my personality. I did everything I could to make people not realize how big I was. I began my journey into personal development and started seeing the difference between a man's world and a woman's world and realized that women who looked better got the better deals, but it still wasn't painful enough for me to do something about it.

Then it almost became easier because of a TV show about Anna Nicole Smith and her weight issues and she became my role model of beauty and big sizes. This is when I realized that I could be fashionable and big. This is when I started matching my big personality with fashionable clothes and most people didn't realize how truly obese I was. My motto at this point was, "I make fat look good." And I did.

However, inside I still felt like that little girl who was bigger than everyone else; the one that had to always try harder because she didn't quite fit in. She wasn't "normal" and didn't deserve what all the skinny girls got.

As I continued to age I also realized that my body was breaking down because of my weight, which was exasperating other issues that had nothing to do with my weight. And I kept trying to convince my husband and my mother that I needed weight-loss surgery and they were totally against it, but they eventually gave in because I was so adamant that I needed it.

In 2014 I had the gastric sleeve, which opened up a whole new world to me. I only lost 50 pounds on it, but it also sparked a new journey for me of wanting to get fit and alleviate all my ailments, which I did. I also began a new journey of working out 5 days week when I was in town and visiting my doctor every 3 months religiously to check my labs and make any modifications I needed to my diet or vitamins to ensure that I stayed healthy.

Now that I've become educated in what healthy is for my body, I know that I could have lost that weight without going through such a drastic procedure. However, I don't regret my decision. It started helping me to transform and feel like I could get my sexy back. And today I'm still struggling with the last 20 pounds that I want to lose, but I finally found a balance that allows me to enjoy eating and still fit into a size

10 comfortably.

Most importantly, my journey has helped me realize that no matter your size, you can feel beautiful, if you allow yourself to feel it and make efforts for yourself—dressing up, wearing makeup, doing your hair, etc. And when you do feel beautiful or even sexy, a lot of times you'll start making slightly healthier choices that will make you healthier overall.

No matter your size, don't give up on yourself. Don't disconnect with that "better you" that you have inside of you. We each have a light inside of us but we allow it to get buried with things we feel are more important than ourselves—our children, our husbands, our jobs—but what we don't realize is that we are damaging ourselves as women permanently in the process. You matter, and you are beautiful, invest in you and enjoy your life.

20

WHEN OPPORTUNITY KNOCKS

ORLY AMOR

About the Author:

Orly Amor always enjoyed speaking and helping people change their lives and impact their circle of influence wherever they go. She was in Property Management for 25 years where she quickly established herself as a Subject Matter Expert; publishing two books on the subject and  speaking on numerous occasions, but she did not feel that she was having an impact.

In 2006, Orly was asked to speak at a woman's shelter on her life experiences and originally declined the invitation. It was there she met a woman who wanted to end her life. After hearing Orly speak the woman decided to live and asked Orly to support her. This was the impact Orly was looking for.

Since then, Orly dedicated her life to impacting the lives

of 200,000,000 people by helping them realize their own mission-based goals and dreams. Her extensive experience as a Certified Behavioral Analyst has made her indispensable as a coach to many influential corporate leaders.

Orly has earned both an MBA and Law Degree. Despite the impressive education and success as a business woman, Orly remains remarkably humble, authentic and a very engaging speaker.

In addition to being a great public speaker herself, and a great networker for the past ten years, she has helped Public Speakers create their Business Model for Public Speaking. Her gift is to show them how to monetize their craft by taking it seriously and having what she calls "Business in A Box for Public Speakers." Thereby teaching them how to fish.

Website: www.OrlyAmor.com

When Opportunity Knocks

"When Opportunity Knocks, Say YES and Figure it out later." – Sir Richard Brunson

I am told I do too much, get too many projects and events going at the same time, too many companies to handle by myself and so on and so on.

I go back to my virtual mentor Sir Richard Brunson who owns over 300 Companies or is involved in many companies and it fascinates me. How does he do it?

Many of my friends, colleagues and family members are saying the same thing about me. How does she do it? Or ask me directly how do you do it?

I think back on my mission and purpose which came clear to me in 2010 where my business coach at the time told me to write down what my personal mission is? I responded without hesitation "I would like to impact the lives of 200,000,000 (Two Hundred Million) People in the next 10 to 20 years." He responded, "you need to be more specific." I said "ok, I will meet you half way. By 2025." He replied, "You need to put a date on it Orly" so I said "Ok, by April 24th, 2025." Knowing in my heart he was expecting me to say by January 1st, 2025.

It is amazing what happens when you have a very clear vision and mission for your personal and your professional life, because all that you need to manifest that vision and mission starts to manifest and come into your life unexpectedly or expectedly if you know and believe in the Law of Attraction. So here we were in January 2010 when I made that declaration about my personal and business mission and vision.

In June of 2010, before I ever considered coaching public speakers on the business of public speaking, I attended and spoke at a conference in Arlington, TX. During one of the breaks I went to the speakers break room for some tea. While I was standing there, three speakers approached me. One of them said *"aren't you Orly Amor?"* I felt very badly because I did not recognize him, so I said *"I'm sorry, do I know you? I really don't remember."* He said *"no we have not officially met before, but I've seen you on the circuit. That's how I know who you are."*

All four of us became engaged in conversation and one of them asked, *"just out of curiosity, how did you get this gig?"*

I replied as if it were common practice, *"I called; I told them what I speak about; they paid, so I'm here!"*

All three of them looked at me as if I had three heads and said, *"You got paid?"* I responded *"Yes, didn't you?"*

They replied, *"we got our **expenses** paid but **we** did not get paid."* I said, *"Oh, I got my expenses AND I got paid."*

All three looked at me and said, *"We want to know how you did it?"* and I jokingly said, *"If I tell you I will have to charge you."* Without hesitation, all 3 said, *"**Name your price.**"* I was floored.

I asked one of them to show me his Speaker Sheet and he

said, *"What is that?"*

I asked, *"Do you have a flier or something you show event planners to get booked?"* and he said, *"Oh, a Media Sheet."*

He gave me a beautiful 4-page folded flier printed on 8.5 x 11 glossy paper. I looked it over for about 10 seconds and said, *"this is garbage."*

He was so insulted, *"what do you mean? I paid over $500 to get this done by a professional!!"*

I responded, *"I understand that, but the event planner won't even look at your name before it hits the garbage can."*

I continued *"There was a survey done of the 100 most stressful jobs in America. Number one was Cardiologist. Number five was Event Planner. Do you actually think that they have the time to read all that you have put into this 4-page flyer? Do you think they have the time to search for your topics and contact information? The answer is No."*

On my way back to New York where I was to meet a client, I was thinking about the conversation with those guys and it came to me "maybe that is what's missing in the industry, maybe speakers just don't know how to do the business side." My heart and mind started racing at the same time.

"The How is Not Your Business." – Les Brown

I remembered the declaration of my mission back in January 2010 where I want to impact the lives of 200,000,000 People by the 24th of April 2025 and it hit me. If I help Public

Speakers, Authors and Coaches how to get paid and make money from Public Speaking and get their message into the masses, we can all do it together. Suddenly the vision and the mission became clear. How I was going to do it was never discussed, but in the back of my mind I was panicking. That quote form Les Brown just jumped into my mind and there was the opportunity of how I was going to achieve that.

Fast forward into 2013 I was offered an opportunity with an organization to run and start a chapter in NYC. This organization was started on the west coast and I was introduced to the founder by a friend. At the time it seemed like a great idea and just another opportunity to connect with people.

At this time, you need to know that when I take on a mandate I will give it my hundred percent and make sure it is a success no matter what? Unfortunately, people in my circle were becoming jealous of my success and used my kindness against me as a weakness. I pressed on despite their attempts to bring me down by starting rumors and just ill intentioned.

Fast forward into the end of 2014, I had just been blindsided by the founder of that organization and a business colleague and a close friend both of which conspired together and just pulled the rug from under me. They shut me down and out. It was not only ill intentioned but done maliciously. The reason I did not see it coming is because I am not like that and I would never cause any harm to another human being. My father God Bless his soul always said "you are too naïve when it comes to people. Not everyone is nice and not everyone is your friend. Stop sharing your success with people."

Sometimes I do think about that conversation with my dad. I told him then and I will tell you now "I will not change who I am." I know that there are also good people out there and the ones that will come into my life also. I look forward to those types of people.

After my colleague and friend and the founder of that organization pulled the rug from under me, I was devastated. One of my closest friends Hara, said "just start your own thing." I thought it was a good idea but what? How? Where? Just wanting to answer those questions was overwhelming.

I went to a chamber of commerce networking event and saw what seemed to be a nightmare in networking. There was segregation. Health and wellness professionals on one side of the room and corporate professionals on the other side of the room. I thought exactly of what was the problem? Those two spheres need to communicate with each other. They are missing countless of opportunities to do business with each other and to help each other grow each other's businesses. I went home frustrated and exhilarated at the same time. I thought of what Hara said and decided to create a mastermind where I would invite a few people from each sphere to meet once a month and connect and help each other while increasing their spheres of influence and grow their respective businesses.

Well, being in New York for now over four years, I realized

that New Yorkers are very last minute, so I decided to create a mastermind on MeetUp.com and put the event as a networking event in 10 days on Eventbrite.com and send one email to my contact list to see what happens.

The day before the event only five people signed up and I was very happy. Because the last-minute people would probably sign up the day of and if 10 or 12 people show up that is a great mastermind group. So I thought.

The day of the event, one of my girlfriends from Pennsylvania dropped by to surprise me as she was in town anyway for another event the next day. As I am setting up for my first mastermind, people started showing up and to my shocking surprise over 62 people showed up. I asked my girlfriend to help with registration and I became the hostess making introductions to people in the room and running around like a chicken with no head.

After about 30 minutes of open networking, I asked everyone to take their seat and told them my mission and vision to what is called the Health and Wellness Network of Commerce Corporation Inc. Its mission is to be a platform for health and wellness professionals, practitioners, product and service providers to network with corporate professionals while providing a sustainable system for both. While I explained my own vision and mission I said the following:

"Ladies and gentlemen, thank you for coming here tonight in such a great number. Some of you I know and some I don't, but I really did not expect this great number of people to show up for a mastermind. So, we are going to treat this first time as a networking event. Please put away your cell phones for just the next 30 minutes and listen to each other. You will each introduce yourself in 30 Seconds in the way that I will instruct you to. Afterwards, when we go back to the open networking section of this event you will see how the energy in this room will go through the roof. We are all here to support each other and we are here to Serve not to Sell."

Everyone got to introduce themselves and afterwards it was exactly as I said the energy was so loud I could hardly hear myself think. At this point everyone is networking and I am catching up with my friend Susan from Pennsylvania. One of the attendees comes up to me and says, "Can I start a group like this in Brooklyn?" I was floored and responded "Huuuu, I don't know, let me think about this." Another girl came up to me and said, "Can I start a group like this in Westchester?" Again, I was floored and replied, "where is Westchester?"

As a side note, I have an MBA and a Law Degree and none of this was coming to me as even a possibility until my girlfriend said "I can start a group like this for you in Punxsutawney, PA." I am floored yet again and then I say "does that place really exist? I remember it from the movie 'Groundhog Day' but I did not know it's a real place?" She said, "yes it does exist." At this point my head is spinning yet again and then I remember both quotes at the same time. The one from Les Brown "The How is Not Your Business" and the one from Sir Richard Brunson "When an opportunity knocks say YES and figure it out later."

I went home that night and wrote not only the business plan but the business model for the Health and Wellness Network of Commerce Corporation Inc. I had to create a Win/Win/Win for the organization, any chapter leader, and all members, individuals and corporate members alike. I got the Website HWNCC up and running and all that starting a business entailed. Guidelines, processes and policies and forms and so on and a month later we were in 3 countries and 3 states. I got all excited as this will be another way by which I impact the lives of 200,000,000 people by the 24th of April 2025.

Today the HWNCC is in 6 countries and 12 states of the USA with over 40 chapters around the world and growing daily. This was all done with no marketing just word of mouth.

So, for all those who say I am crazy to take on another project and or start a new company. I will say in the words of one of my mentors and the author of the foreword to this book, Bert Oliva "crazy people succeed." To those who think and say to me daily that I need to slow down I say, "you need to catch up."

Opportunities knock on our doors every day and all you have to do is say YES!

To Your Ongoing Success

The Authors of This Book have collaborated to bring you their Success Works in order to inspire and motivate you to Never Give Up!

Made in the USA
Middletown, DE
27 November 2018